MAKING HISTORY

MAKiNG

HiSTORY

Have a BLAST with 15 Crafts

CREATIVE PROJECTS FROM THE MINNESOTA HISTORICAL SOCIETY

WENDY FRESHMAN AND KRISTIN JANSSON

PHOTOGRAPHY BY BILL JOLITZ

MINNESOTA
HISTORICAL
SOCIETY PRESS

To Bernadyne Holzman, crafter extraordinaire; and to Phil, Nia, and Noam Freshman, the best "production assistants" and supporters of this project —WF

To cherished friends and family, for whom my handmade gifts are thanks for enriching my life. —KJ

© 2014 by the Minnesota Historical Society. All rights reserved. No part of this book may be used or reproduced in any manner whatsoever without written permission except in the case of brief quotations embodied in critical articles and reviews. For information, write to the Minnesota Historical Society Press, 345 Kellogg Blvd. W., St. Paul, MN 55102-1906.

www.mnhspress.org

The Minnesota Historical Society Press is a member of the Association of American University Presses.

Manufactured in the United States of America

10 9 8 7 6 5 4 3 2 1

♾ The paper used in this publication meets the minimum requirements of the American National Standard for Information Sciences—Permanence for Printed Library Materials, ANSI Z39.48-1984.

International Standard Book Number
ISBN: 978-0-87351-919-9 (paper)

Library of Congress Cataloging-in-Publication Data
Freshman, Wendy, author.
    Making history : have a blast with 15 crafts, creative projects from the Minnesota Historical Society / Wendy Freshman and Kristin Jansson.
        pages cm
    Audience: Ages 8+.
    ISBN 978-0-87351-919-9 (pbk. : alk. paper)
1. Handicraft—Juvenile literature. 2. Minnesota—History—Juvenile literature. I. Jansson, Kristin, author. II. Title.
    TT857.F74 2014
    745.59—dc23
                                        2014021282

Templates on pages 176–206 available for downloading at www.mnhspress.org/makinghistory, where you can also view a fun video about making the North Woods Troll (see page 11).

CONTENTS

Introduction 1
   Notes about Skill Levels.. 3
   Notes about Supplies... 5
   Acknowledgments... 9

CREATURE AND PEOPLE CRAFTS
North Woods Troll 11
Playful Marionette.. 17

WEARABLE CRAFTS
Metal Foil Repoussé Pendant................................. 27
Nifty '50s Apron 35
Hmong Rooster Comb Hat 43
Minnesota Trapper Hat 51

HOME KITS AND DECORATIONS
Makak Generation Basket 63
Civil War Sewing Kit 75

JUST FOR FUN
"Gone Fishing" Ice House..................................... 83
Burning Spear Story Staff 97
Cobweb Valentine 107
Día de los Muertos Nicho..................................... 119

MOVING CRAFTS
"Ride the Waves" Boat and Skier 129
Paul Bunyan Action Toy 145
Twister Tornado.. 159

Templates 176

MAKiNG HiSTORY

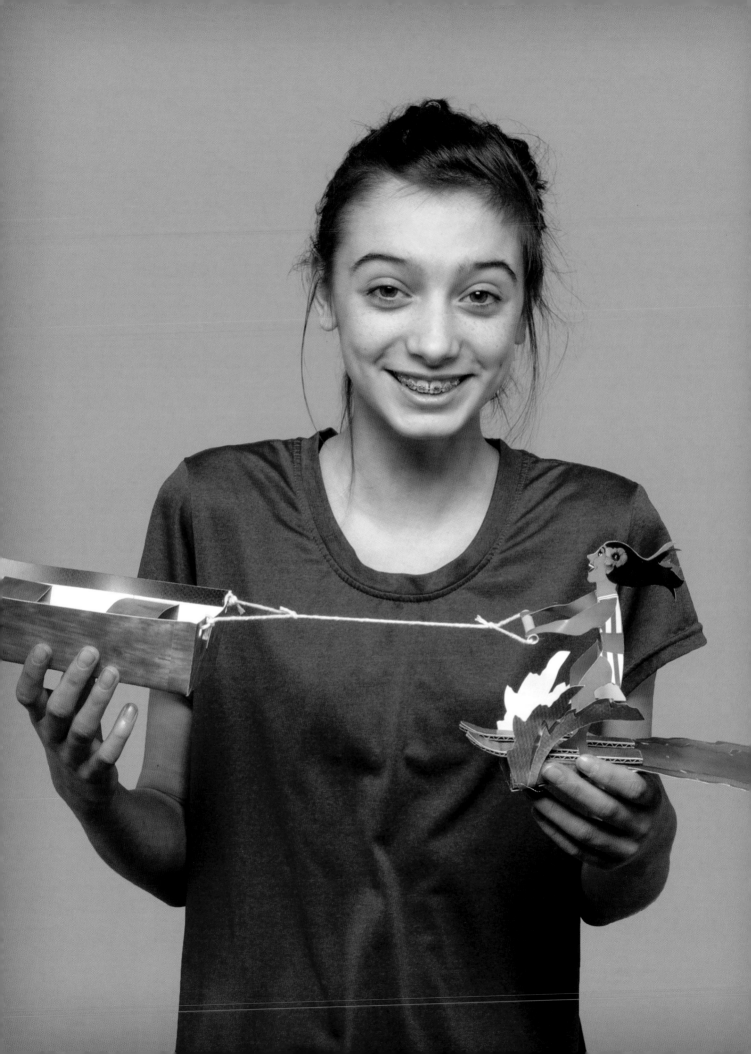

INTRODUCTION

T his is a craft book with a distinct Minnesota flavor. It features engaging projects tied to Minnesota history and culture that are made from easily found materials. Each craft has detailed step-by-step directions with patterns and templates for creating parts and pieces. There are also helpful hints and photos to guide you along the way as you create.

When we began brainstorming for the book, in the spring of 2013, we discovered that both of us had grown up in families with a fearless attraction to making stuff. Laying out and cutting a magician's cape? "No problem." Making a pair of stilts? "Let's try it." As kids we were both lucky to have role models who taught us that there's nothing more satisfying than figuring out how to create something with your own hands. And we knew we could always ask for help.

Now we are both parents. Our kids have grown up to become impressive makers and builders, and we can clearly see that crafting is a gift passed on through generations. The fun (and sometimes frustration) of making a project is in "the doing." The delightful benefit of working as a team to share the experience and discovery is also part of the fun, as is the ultimate satisfaction of finishing the job.

The projects we picked reflect Minnesota stories, and legends about people, and things that make us smile. There's a Lake Pepin water-skier pulled behind a boat that actually glides. You'll find a twisting tornado inspired by real funnel clouds that hit Rochester in 1883. And you can create a north woods troll made of sticks and leaves. Many of the crafts are inspired by handmade objects. They represent a wide range of cultures and artistry that are found in the Minnesota Historical Society's museum collections. These include Civil War–era sewing kits, Hmong textiles, 1950s-style aprons, and trapper hats. The crafts also represent Victorian-era valentines, needlework patterns, Ojibwe birch-bark baskets, and the junk genius of African American folk artist Maurice Carlton.

If objects tell stories (and we think they do), then we hope you will have fun learning about these Minnesota artifacts that truly represent both "art" and "fact." We encourage you to add *your* story to the projects. Build on and share what you know as you work on the projects in this book. Add your own special touches, and create together.

Wendy Freshman and Kristin Jansson

NOTES ABOUT SKILL LEVELS

Projects are labeled according to skill level or complexity, from 1 (easiest) to 4 (hardest or most complex). However, don't let this scare you away from level 4 projects. When you break down a project into steps, all of them are doable. Harder ones require more patience or time. But with an adult, older friend, or sibling's help, you'll be well on your way to making an awesome project!

Skill Level 1

Skills include: cutting, gluing, decorating

- North Woods Troll
- Hmong Rooster Comb Hat

Skill Level 2

Skills include: cutting paper and felt, embossing metal foil, cutting and using duct tape, gluing, coloring, decorating with 3-D objects, measuring

- Playful Marionette
- Metal Foil Repoussé Pendant
- Civil War Sewing Kit
- Burning Spear Story Staff
- Cobweb Valentine

Skill Level 3

Skills include: cutting some complex shapes, measuring, gluing, decorating, making 3-D objects, cutting and using duct tape, pleating

- Nifty '50s Apron
- Makak Generation Basket
- "Gone Fishing" Ice House
- Día de Los Muertos Nicho
- "Ride the Waves" Boat and Skier

Skill Level 4

Skills include: cutting, measuring, stapling, cutting corrugated cardboard, complex assembly, adjusting parts, bending wire

- Minnesota Trapper Hat
- Paul Bunyan Action Toy
- Twister Tornado

Adult Help:

Some steps in these crafts are best done as a team. An adult should help with hot glue guns, as well as using pins, cutting tough cardboard, and so on. When assistance is recommended in the instructions, the words **Adult Help** will appear. Kids should ask for help at this stage.

General rules:

- Read the directions first. It's really helpful to look through the pictures so you and your parents have some idea what is involved.
- Make sure you have the time and the supplies you need.
- Ask for adult help when you see the adult icon.
- Use sharp scissors with care.
- Be responsible and keep small and dangerous things out of the hands of little brothers or sisters.
- Ask for help when you think a step is confusing or you have trouble doing it. An older person can help you figure out a good way to do it. It's not fun to make things when you're frustrated.
- Cover your work area. And clean up when you finish!
- Try new skills. It will make you feel great about yourself.

NOTES ABOUT SUPPLIES

We like to keep it simple. You might read a supply list for a craft in this book and think you have materials at home that could do the same job. Check with your parents to help you decide if it's a good substitute. If so, feel free to use what you already have, unless the supply list asks for something specific (like 18-gauge wire).

GLUE

Artists who make 3-D objects talk about glue when they put things together. In fact, whole books have been written about the subject! Some things just stick together better with one glue than another. We will tell you in the supply list if you need a certain kind. But if we don't say "hot glue" or Gorilla Glue, then usually it doesn't matter. Glue sticks are easier to use for large areas, especially the ones that go on purple and dry clear.

✔ **TIP:** Experiment to see which glue works best, is not too messy, and has a quick "grab."

Here are some glues that we think work well:

- Scotch brand Quick-Dry Adhesive (made by 3M, a Minnesota company)
- Aleene's Tacky Glue (You can sometimes find 1-ounce bottles, a great size for gluing small areas. Tiny glue tips make it easy!)
- Gorilla Glue for attaching plastic toys and other non-porous materials
- Regular white school glue

✔ **TIP:** Old magazines can be very helpful in avoiding a mess when using glue. Open the magazine and use the pages as your work area. This way glue will drip on the magazine instead of the table. Just turn the page when you need a clean, dry spot.

✔ **TIP:** Place a damp rag or washcloth on a plate (not on your nice wood table) to keep handy while you glue. Clean fingers keep unwanted glue off your projects!

HOT GLUE GUN AND HOT MELT GLUE

Hot glue guns and hot melt glue are great to use when strong hold is needed. They are often the best choice to glue cardboard together because the glue "grabs" so fast and dries quickly. But you need to be careful! Always have an adult help you use hot glue. It can burn you and be very messy if you're not careful. Here are some tips to make hot glue use safer and easier:

- There are "hi-temp" and "lo-temp" hot glues. The lo-temp will work for all of the projects in this book that call for hot glue, and it's safer for children.

- Always, always unplug the gun when you leave the room.

- Always make sure to keep electric cords out of the way. Kicking a cord by accident can send a glue gun flying!

- Practice hot gluing on a scrap piece of cardboard before you use a glue gun in any craft. As the glue gun gets warmer, the glue flows easier.

✔ **TIP:** Using a hot glue gun is easier, safer, and less messy if you make a holder for it.

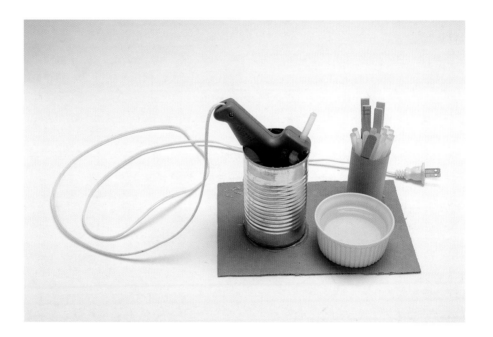

- **Adult Help:** Take an empty, clean, 15-ounce tin can. Have an adult help you hot glue it to a piece of cardboard. This will act as a holder. You can set the hot glue gun in the can when you aren't using it. It will keep the hot end safe and keep the handle ready to grab when you need it.

- Glue on a cardboard toilet paper tube to hold extra hot melt glue sticks. Trim it shorter than the glue sticks to make them easy to grab.

- Place a small dish of water next to the tin can. (A clean, empty, round tuna fish can works great.) If you accidentally get glue on your fingers, immediately dip them in the cool water so you don't get burned. We attached the dish and cardboard together with adhesive Velcro. That keeps it in place but also makes it easy to empty the water.

CARDBOARD

- Lots of projects in this book call for cardboard. Corrugated cardboard is the kind most shipping boxes are made from. If you look at it closely, you'll see that there are ridges, or a ripply paper, in between two layers. That makes it stronger. Some corrugated cardboard is very heavy or stiff, but you don't need to use it for these crafts. And if you have trouble cutting out pieces, you can always ask for help.

- If there are other cardboards we want you to use, they will be named in the supply list. Cereal boxes, gift boxes, and poster board are examples. You should be able to make most of the projects with scrap cardboard around your house. It's a good way to recycle!

SCISSORS

- Sharp scissors make cutting so much easier! Long-bladed scissors cut nice straight lines. Smaller scissors are useful for smaller or curved areas or detailed facial features.

- Match the weight of the scissors to the material you're cutting. Use a heavier weight (or bigger) scissors for plastic or cardboard. Don't use a delicate embroidery scissors for cutting cardboard! You will ruin the blade.

- Don't use fabric scissors for these crafts, either. The paper and cardboard you will be cutting can dull the blades very quickly, and they won't cut fabric very well after that.

- We like Fiskars brand. They offer lots of different shapes, sizes, and weights. You can also buy a Fiskars sharpener to keep the scissors working well.

✔ **TIP:** When you cut the templates or cardboard shapes, it's easier if you roughly cut a wide shape around them first. Once some of the paper or cardboard has been cut away, you can get closer to the outline.

SCORING TOOLS

We score fold lines on paper and cardboard projects in order to bend the material accurately and easily. There are several kinds of scoring tools. Use what's handy.

- Bone folder. This is the traditional bookbinder's tool. Once they were made from bone, but now they're often made from plastic or Teflon.

- A butter knife (a small knife with a smooth edge) or the dull side of a table knife.

OTHER USEFUL SUPPLIES

- Clamps. Spring-loaded clothespins or small plastic clamps you can get at the hardware store help hold pieces together while you glue or assemble something.

- Hole punches. We list two kinds, a ¼-inch and an ⅛-inch punch. You can get them at most craft stores. If you don't have an ⅛-inch punch, use other things to poke a hole instead. A small nail, awl, or leather punch can all be used. Ask for adult help, and protect your work surface.

■ Cutting mats. These protect your work surface. Always use one when cutting with an X-Acto knife or box cutter!

■ See-through quilter's rulers are great. People who work in costume shops use them all the time. It's much easier to mark lines because you can see what is underneath. You can get them at craft or art supply stores and fabric shops.

TEMPLATES

Many projects in this book involve templates for tracing or copying. Templates start on page 176, and they are also available online at www.mnhspress.org/makinghistory. If you have a computer, Internet access, and a printer, you can make as many copies of the templates as you like. You can also take the templates to a copy store to have larger versions made.

✔ **TIP:** Many of these crafts ask you to print a template on card stock. If your home printer is a roller-style printer, it may not be able to handle card stock. Instead, you can print the templates on regular printing paper and then use a glue stick to glue the printed templates onto card stock.

If you don't have card stock, matte photo paper (also called presentation paper or double-sided matte paper) can also be used. The only craft that requires heavy-weight paper of your choice is the water-skier. She needs sturdy legs to help her ski!

✔ **TIP:** Have fun and enjoy the projects!

ACKNOWLEDGMENTS

Custom step-by-step photography by the indefatigable, accommodating, and ever-cheerful Bill Jolitz (and thanks to Eric Mortenson at the Minnesota Historical Society for photo studio space).

Thanks to MNHS Press interns who assisted in the process: Elizabeth Black, Jamie Crowson, Abby Erickson, Fue Yang, and Jaime Zyvoloski.

Crafty consultants: Marlin Heise, Pat Kruse, Karen Lehman, Linda McShannock, Mary Kay Nutzmann, Kate Roberts, Christina Washam, and Shoua Vang Xiong with the Hmong ABC Bookstore in St. Paul.

And to our charming and photogenic models: Elizabeth Black, Aliya Booker, Isabella Crowson, William Crowson, Weston Danks, Lux Fabre, Mariela Frias, Solisa Frias, Avi Hennen, Alvin Leary, Frank Leary, Alex Mayhew, Evie Nold, Edgar Ockuly, Avery Sellers, Le'elage Sellers, Pashoua Vang, Lee Yolei Yang, and Jaime Zyvoloski. Thanks also to their assorted family members, for whiling away a Saturday or two with us in the studio.

Thanks to Adam Demers and Andrea Leap for providing introductions that led to this craft collaboration.

Love and thanks to our husbands for their patience and good humor as they endured a year of mounting craft debris.

And finally, our appreciation goes to the staff at MNHS Press for their confidence and bravery as they offered two neophytes this project, carte blanche. This book would not have been possible without their wisdom, creativity, enthusiasm, and guidance. Our grateful thanks to Shannon Pennefeather, Dan Leary, Mary Poggione, Alison Aten, and Pam McClanahan.

Credits

page 11 Troll image from iStock

page 64 Photo courtesy of Bockley Gallery, Minneapolis

page 64 *My Brother's Blanket #3*, 2010, 38 × 36 inches. Collection: Plains Art Museum, Fargo. Photo courtesy of Bockley Gallery, Minneapolis.

page 83 Ice house origin story courtesy Tom Uehling

page 188 Fish in the template courtesy National Oceanic and Atmospheric Administration/Department of Commerce

Except where noted, all historical photographs are from the collections of the Minnesota Historical Society

North Woods Troll; Minnesota Trapper Hat; "Gone Fishing" Ice House; "Ride the Waves" Boat and Skier; and Paul Bunyan Action Toy template illustration and design by Kristin Jansson

Hmong Rooster Comb Hat template assistance by Christina Washam

Cobweb Valentine template assistance by Jaime Zyvoloski

Día de los Muertos skeleton images by Therese Scheller

NORTH WOODS TROLL

Skill Level 1

"Is that a face?" your friend whispers as you walk in the woods.

"Are you crazy?" you say. "That's just a tree!"

But then you look again, and you see it, too: a long crooked nose, knobby fingers, hair blowing in the wind.

Suddenly your hair stands on end. Everywhere you look, you see faces: in the trees, in the rocks and clouds, even in the tree roots. It's as if the woods are teeming with grotesque creatures.

"Trolls!" you scream. "Run!"

Trolls are mythical beings who originated in the rugged landscape of Scandinavia, where they live to this day, hidden in nature. They are as varied in appearance as humans themselves. Sometimes they resemble trees, mountains, or stones. Other times they appear to be more human, but with long noses and tails, or multiple heads! Trolls are smelly and disagreeable. They are dim witted, ugly, strong, and stubborn. They cause trouble wherever they roam. But they are no match for a child's courage, kindness, and resourcefulness.

People from all cultures have stories about mythical creatures living around them. These creatures often represent the dark side of human nature. Stories in which people interact with imaginary creatures teach us a lot about what it means to be human. Children facing these creatures learn how to rely on themselves. They learn how to be smart and bounce back from difficult situations.

When people from different lands move to a new country, they bring their stories with them. Those stories reflect a culture's values and its history. Stories of trolls arrived in Minnesota with Scandinavian immigrants. Large numbers of Scandinavians moved to the state following the passage of the Homestead

Trunk made in Norway in 1825 and brought to Minnesota. Perhaps it carried some Old World traditions as well.

11

Act of 1862. Through this act, the U.S. government gave 160 acres of land to anyone who would live on and farm the land for five years. Within three years, 75,000 people moved to Minnesota. That adds up to a lot of people with stories about trolls!

In this craft, you'll make your very own troll. Natural objects you collect will help your troll blend in with the outdoors where you live.

Supplies

- ☐ **Adult Help:** Troll Bark and Troll Base templates (page 176 or at www.mnhspress.org /makinghistory), photocopied or printed on card stock or matte photo paper (see note page 8)

- ☐ Lightweight cardboard (cereal box, poster board, or manila folder)

- ☐ Scissors

- ☐ Glue stick

- ☐ Craft glue

- ☐ **Adult Help:** Hot glue gun and hot melt glue

- ☐ Butter knife or bone folder

- ☐ Ruler

- ☐ Small clamp or spring-loaded clothespin

- ☐ An assortment of twigs, with or without leaves

  ✔ **TIP:** Good troll twigs have a center stick with two twigs on either side to form arms. It's great if the center stick also has a nose. (See above for an example.)

- ☐ Beads or small pebbles for eyes

- ☐ Optional, if you want to add hair: yarn, leaves, acorn hats, bark, or string

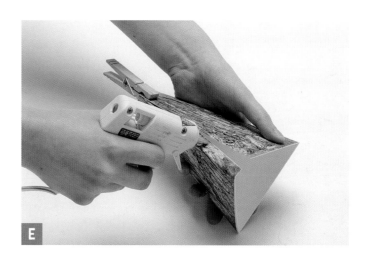

Directions

MAKE THE TROLL BASE

- Roughly cut out the Troll Base template. You will trim it later, so it doesn't need to be exact. Leave the Troll Bark for later. **A**

- Glue the printed Troll Base template onto lightweight cardboard with a glue stick. Make sure you coat the whole piece before you stick them together. Lay a heavy book on top of it and let it dry for about 5 minutes before you cut and fold it. **B**

- After the glue is dry, cut out the Troll Base.

- Look for the fold lines on the Base. For each one, place the ruler on the line. Use a butter knife or bone folder to score it by pressing the fold line firmly right on the line. This should indent, *but not cut through,* the card stock. This step makes it easier to fold. Repeat on all fold lines. **C**

- Fold each fold line on the Base. It will become a cone shape. The design should be on the outside of the cone. There will be an opening at the top of the cone. **D**

- Look for the narrow flap on one side. Tuck the flap underneath the third side. You can use a clothespin to clamp the sides together at the top of the cone to help hold it while you glue.

- **Adult Help:** Have an adult help you use the hot glue gun to glue the small flap underneath the third side. **E**

- Remove the clothespin.

Now you're ready to turn this cone into a troll. This is the fun part. You get to decide how your troll will look. Each troll will look different, depending on the materials you decide to use. You can choose to use the printed Bark from the template, or twigs, bark, weeds, or grass you gathered. Remember, trolls need to blend in with their natural surroundings!

MAKE THE TROLL FEATURES

▦ Take the twig that you want to use for the body/head/arms and stick it into the opening at the top of the cone-shaped Base. **F**

▦ If the stick is slightly wider than the opening, use a scissors to cut the opening a little larger. Don't worry if it looks a little messy. You can cover this area with the Troll Bark later.

▦ **Adult Help:** Ask an adult to help you glue the stick in place with a glue gun. **G**

▦ Cut out Bark pieces from the template. You can cut and use them all or just a few pieces. Don't worry about cutting them out exactly. Bark can be any shape.

▦ Fold and bend some of the pieces down the middle. This gives them a 3-D effect. **H**

▦ **Adult Help:** Use the craft glue or hot glue to attach pieces of the Bark onto the cone body. Place them wherever you like.

✔ **TIP:** Glue just the top edge of a piece of Bark and leave the rest hanging loose on the cone. This adds more texture, making the troll more interesting. You can glue Bark pieces to cover up the neck opening. You can also glue a long piece over each shoulder like a strap.

▦ Add hair if you want. We found a leafy twig and used a glue gun to attach it to the head. You can use yarn or string. You can also use the natural materials you may have gathered, like acorn hats, bark, or grass. **I**

▦ Add eyes. Glue pebbles or beads onto the face with craft glue. Let the glue dry before you play with it. **J**

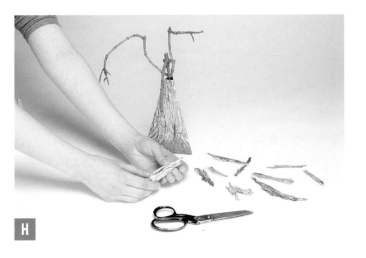

When you're happy with the way your troll looks, you're done. Have fun playing with it. But don't lose your troll in the woods. They love to hide!

Make a whole family of trolls. Enlarge or reduce the Troll Base template when you print it. You could also trace the base template onto plain lightweight cardboard. Glue real twigs or bark to the cone. (Don't strip bark from living trees! Only use bark you find on the ground.)

PLAYFUL MARIONETTE

Skill Level 2

Have you ever cheered friends up when they were sad or sick by making them something special? Maybe you made some cookies or a beautiful card. Remember how good you felt when you made a difference in their day?

That's what Deborah Meader did in 1927. When her young daughter was sick, Deborah made a simple puppet to entertain her. What happened from there was a surprise. Making puppets became Deborah's career! She also taught others to make and use puppets. This creative job allowed Deborah to help support her family during the Great Depression. This was a time when people living in the United States struggled to earn money.

Minnesota was hit hard by the Great Depression in the 1930s. Twenty-five percent of people did not have jobs. President Roosevelt wanted to help create jobs for people, so he established the Works Progress Administration (WPA). Its goal was to provide people with jobs and paychecks. It would also train leaders and workers to work together efficiently.

Deborah was the State Supervisor of Puppetry for the Minnesota WPA from 1935 to 1941. She believed puppetry was a perfect tool to carry out these goals. She believed it was a democratic art form, that it was art for everyone. Puppetry brought people with different skills together to create something meaningful. She employed and taught many people as she took her puppets to state hospitals, libraries, schools, churches, and prisons.

In addition to her work with the WPA, Deborah also started her own business in St. Paul. She made and sold puppets, plays, and portable puppet stages that she designed. She did all this at a time when very few women worked in jobs outside their homes.

Just think—it all started with a simple puppet made to entertain a sick child.

You can make your own puppet to cheer people up. Here are directions to make a marionette, a puppet that you move with strings. You will use simple

Puppets for Works Progress Administration puppet shows, 1935

17

supplies: felt, cardboard, a pair of shoelaces, and a photo. The photo is the fun part—it will be the face of your puppet. It can be of a friend, family member, or pet.

Supplies

- ☐ **Adult Help:** Marionette Body, Shoe Front, Shoe Back, Shoe Sole, and Control Bar templates (page 177 or at www.mnhspress.org/makinghistory), photocopied or printed on card stock (see note page 8)

- ☐ 2 (9 × 12–inch) pieces of adhesive-backed felt (found at craft stores or online)

- ☐ Piece of corrugated cardboard (10 × 10 inches)

- ☐ Marker

- ☐ ⅛–inch hole punch or a tool to make a small hole

- ☐ A pair of thin shoelaces 45 inches or longer

- ☐ Ruler

- ☐ Scissors

- ☐ 4 size ⁵⁄₁₆–inch flat washers

- ☐ **Adult Help:** Hot glue gun and hot melt glue

- ☐ Glue stick or craft glue

- ☐ Flattened cereal box

- ☐ Manila folder, lightweight cardboard, or index cards

- ☐ Masking tape or Washi Tape (decorative tape, available at craft stores)

- ☐ Straight pins

- ☐ 2 identical close-up copies of a photo, such as a school photo, to use for the marionette's face

   ✔ **TIP:** The photo should match the size of the template face, but a little bigger or smaller won't matter. This will be a permanent feature of your puppet, so use copies of the photo, not the actual photo, if it's important to you or your family. You can also use a magazine face instead, or draw your own.

Optional Supplies

- ☐ Markers
- ☐ Duct tape
- ☐ Ribbons
- ☐ Pom-poms
- ☐ Stickers

Directions

PREPARE THE TEMPLATES

- Cut out the Marionette Body, Shoe Front, Shoe Back, Shoe Sole, and Control Bar templates.
- Punch holes in the knees of the Body template as marked. Set all templates aside.

MAKE THE BODY

- Remove the backing from one piece of adhesive-backed felt. Lay it on the table with the sticky side up.
- Remove the backing from the second piece of felt.
- **Adult Help:** Ask an adult to help you carefully lay the second piece—sticky side down—on top of the first piece. The sticky sides should face each other.

  ✔ **TIP:** It is helpful to ask an adult to help you stick the felt pieces together because they stick fast and hard. You only get one chance!

- Smooth the felt pieces with your hands to make sure they are stuck together everywhere.
- Take the Body template and use a marker to trace its outline onto the felt. Cut out the felt body.
- Place a dot on the felt to match the punched knee holes on the template. Use the ⅛-inch punch to make one hole at each dot.

MAKE THE SHOES

■ Trace the Shoe Front and Shoe Back templates onto corrugated cardboard. You will need to trace four copies of each. Cut them out.

■ Trace the Shoe Sole template on the cereal box cardboard. You will need four copies. Cut them out.

■ **Adult Help:** Lay one of the cardboard shoe soles on your work surface. Ask an adult to help you hot glue two flat washers to the top of the sole. Glue one washer in front of the other. **C**

■ **Adult Help:** Place a second shoe sole on top of the washers. Line it up by matching the two pointed ends. It should look like a "washer sandwich": a shoe sole on the bottom, washers glued in the middle, and another sole on top. Remove the top sole, squirt hot glue on top of the washers, and replace the top.

■ Repeat the last two steps with the second set of soles and washers. At this point, you should have two "washer sandwiches."

■ **Adult Help:** Next, cover each "washer sandwich" with two layers of corrugated cardboard. Take one shoe front and one shoe back. (One is pointed and one looks like a half circle.) Have an adult help you hot glue them on top of the "washer sandwich" so that the pointed part lines up and the curved back lines up. There will be a small gap in between the two top layers of cardboard. **D**

■ Repeat this step and glue a second pair of shoe fronts and shoe backs onto the same shoe. Set this shoe aside.

■ Make the second shoe in the same way. Now you have two identical shoes.

■ Cover the shoes with layers of masking tape or Washi Tape.

✔ **TIP:** Cover the whole shoe, but leave the gap open. This is where you will glue the leg to the shoe.

ATTACH THE SHOES

- **Adult Help:** Glue the shoe to the bottom of the first leg. Have an adult help you run a line of hot glue along the bottom of the notch in one shoe. Immediately wedge the bottom of the felt leg into the notch. Hold until the glue cools. **E**

    ✔ **TIP:** Your fingers will be very close to the hot glue, so be careful!

- Repeat the last step with the second leg and shoe. If you used masking tape, you can decorate the shoes if you like. Use markers to color them. You can also add little bows or pom-poms.

MAKE THE FACE

- Glue the two copies of the face that you are using onto the lightweight cardboard with a glue stick.

- Cut out both faces. You only need the faces, not the neck. **F**

- Take one of the faces. Make a dot with a marker in the middle of the head, about ¼ inch down from the top. Use the ⅛-inch punch to make a hole there.

- Place the felt marionette body on the table in front of you with the front side facing up. Place the face with the hole on top of it. Move it around until it's pleasing to you.

- Use a straight pin or a piece of masking tape to mark the felt where the bottom of the chin is. This will remind you where it fits when you glue it on. **G**

- If there is extra felt sticking out from behind the face, mark it with a marker so you know where to trim.

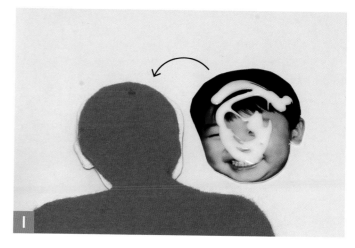

- Move the photo off the body. Trim away the felt that sticks out.

- Place the photo back onto the body, and line up the chin with your tape or pin mark.

- **Adult Help:** Add a tiny dot of hot glue just underneath the chin to hold the photo in place. When the glue cools, gently pull the top edge of the face away from the felt and put a very small amount of glue in a couple places on the felt. Lay the face back down onto the glue and press gently with your fingertips. **H**

- Punch a hole through the felt layer to match the hole in the top of the head.

- Flip the marionette over, face down.

- Take the second face picture and spread a thin layer of craft glue on the front. **I**

  ✔ **TIP:** This picture is a shape template. It will match the shape of the face on the front of the marionette exactly.

- Place the face, *glue side down,* on the back of the felt. Line up the edges with the front face. The felt will be sandwiched between the front and back photos. Press down gently.

- Set aside to dry while you make the control bar.

MAKE THE CONTROL BAR

- Take the Control Bar template and punch holes where the three dots are.

- Lay the Control Bar template on top of a piece of corrugated cardboard. Trace around the template twice so you have two rectangles. Mark the placement of the punched holes on each cardboard piece.

- Cut out the two cardboard control bars. Use a punch to make holes where you have marked the three dots.

- **Adult Help:** Use a glue gun to glue the two cardboard pieces together. Make sure you line up the holes! **J**

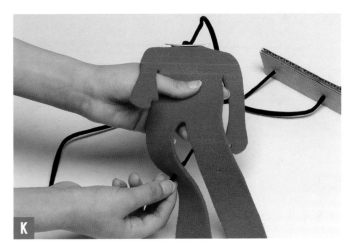

STRING YOUR MARIONETTE

- Take your marionette and make sure the glue on the photo is dry. Punch a hole in the back photo to match the holes that are already there.

- Take your shoelaces and cut each one in half so you have four pieces. Set one piece aside because you won't need it. Now you have three pieces that are the same length.

- Take one piece of shoelace. Use the ruler to measure from the plastic tip. Cut a piece that is 14 inches long.

- Take the other two shoelace pieces. From the plastic tip, measure and cut pieces that are 20 inches long.

- Grab the 14-inch shoelace. Tie a double knot at the cut end.

- Use the plastic tip of the shoelace as a needle. Insert it through the middle hole of the control bar and pull it until the knot reaches the cardboard.

- Insert the plastic tip through the hole in the marionette's head from front to back. Tie it in a knot to secure it to the head. (Or glue or tape it to the back of the head instead.)

- Grab the other two shoelaces and tie a double knot at the cut end of each. Thread one through one of the remaining two holes. Then thread it through the hole in the knee on the same side. Go in through the front of the knee to the back. Tie one knot to secure the shoelace. **K**

- Repeat this step on the other side, threading the shoelace through the remaining hole on the control bar and through the knee. Tie a knot to secure it.

- Check to see if the leg strings are even. Hold up your marionette and let it hang freely from the bar. It will not hang completely straight. It will look like it's about to sit down. **L** (page 24)

- Do the legs and feet look like they are hanging even with each other? If they are not, adjust them by retying the knots behind the knee. When they are hanging evenly, tie the knots a second time to make sure they won't come undone.

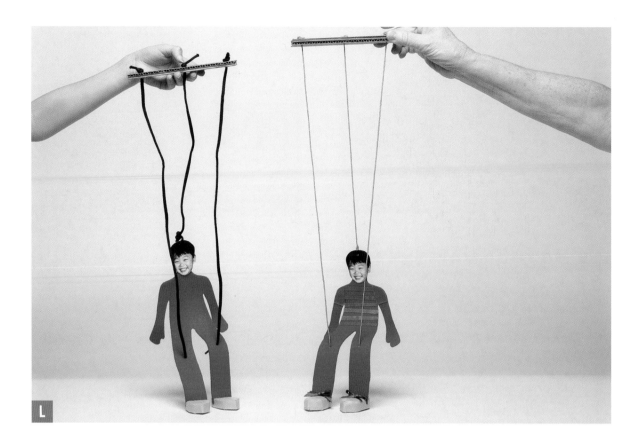

■ Your marionette is complete. If you want to decorate it, you can add tape strips to make stripes, pom-poms, and more.

CONTROLLING YOUR MARIONETTE

■ Now it's time to practice making the marionette move.

■ Lift the marionette up by the control bar. Leave its feet on the floor or table. The puppet will be in a slightly seated position as it hangs.

■ Hold the string for the head in one hand and lift it up slightly so the marionette stands straight. Move the legs with a twisting motion of your other hand. It looks like the marionette is walking. With practice, you can even make it walk up stairs!

If you used the face of a friend or family member on your marionette, show them your creation. We bet you'll make them smile.

METAL FOIL REPOUSSÉ PENDANT

Skill Level 2

I f you know how to embroider, you know that it takes artistic ability, patience, and practice—lots of it! Can you imagine earning a living embroidering cloth? Think about opening an embroidery business. Imagine hiring women to embroider, and then staying in business for over 30 years! Running that business would require many other skills as well.

In the late 1800s, artistic women were not encouraged to become painters, sculptors, or illustrators. They were encouraged to express their creativity in a different way, by making decorative arts for the home. Embroidery was one such art.

But some women wanted to share their art with others, outside their homes. This included two sisters in Hastings, Minnesota, named Alice and Florence LeDuc. Their mother, Mary LeDuc, and their niece, Edith Gardner, joined them. What was their craft? Embroidery! Together these women formed their own company in 1888. It was called Hastings Needlework. The company was in business for more than 34 years. In that time, the women sold over 2,100 pieces of embroidery. Some pieces were sold to the Pillsbury and Hill families, whose members were well known and important in Minnesota. The women's embroidery was featured on magazine covers. It was even included in an exhibition in Paris, France.

Today, more than 800 patterns for Hastings Needlework designs are preserved in the collections of the Minnesota Historical Society. The patterns are great examples of the artistry

Hastings Needlework drawing, circa 1910–1917

of the women who created them. In this craft, you'll use one of these historic patterns. But you won't need a needle! You'll use one of Alice LeDuc's elegant designs to create a unique necklace.

The necklace pendant will be made from metal foil. You will use an ancient art technique called *repoussé*. Its name comes from the word *repousser*. In French, this means "to push" or "to emboss." Repoussé artwork is a raised, textured design created from a flat piece of metal. The metal is first placed on top of a pot of pitch. Pitch is a wood tar, or asphalt material. The pitch indents slightly as the artist works on the metal, and it supports the metal. Design lines are engraved onto the metal surface. The artist then flips the metal piece over and hammers it from the back. The hammering gently stretches and pushes the metal into the pitch. This forms a raised area on the front that is the shape of the

Hastings Needlework drawing, circa 1910–1917

design. The artist flips the metal piece back to the front to deepen the engraving lines, then flips it again to hammer. Engrave, hammer, engrave, hammer. This happens many times before it is finished.

This craft will follow a similar process, but simplified. Your repoussé necklace pendant will be made using many common household items. You will use pencil erasers and cotton swabs to form the raised design. Your engraving tools will be pens and pencils. Your "pitch" will be a piece of fun foam. This craft uses a design from the Hastings Needlework company. Both embroidery and repoussé create beautifully textured surfaces, but your metal foil craft will be easier and quicker to make.

Supplies

- ☐ Repoussé Pendant Design template (page 178 or at www.mnhspress.org/makinghistory), copied or printed on standard paper

- ☐ 36-gauge metal foil (available at art supply or hobby stores, or online)

    ✔ **TIP:** You will only need a piece that is 4 × 3 inches, but it's nice to have some extra so that you can practice—or make more than one.

- ☐ Flattened cereal box or lightweight cardboard

- ☐ Scissors

- ☐ Dull pencil with eraser

- ☐ Medium-point pen

- ☐ Cotton swabs

- ☐ Foam sheet (available at craft stores)

☐ Masking tape

☐ Ruler

☐ ⅛– or ¼–inch hole punch

☐ A piece of string (can be silk cord, yarn, thin ribbon, or shoelace) long enough to tie both ends as well as go over your head easily

☐ 2–4 beads with holes big enough to fit string

Optional Supplies

☐ Tempera paint

☐ Paintbrush

☐ Liquid shoe polish

☐ Rag or cotton ball

☐ Fine-point permanent marker

Directions

MAKE THE PENDANT

▪ On the cardboard, measure and mark a rectangle that is 3½ × 2½ inches. Cut it out and set aside.

▪ Take the 36-gauge metal foil and a pen. Measure and mark a rectangle that is 4 × 3 inches. Cut it out and set aside.

✔ **TIP: Adult Help:** Be careful when you cut! The metal can be sharp.

▪ Take the cardboard rectangle you cut. Center it over the metal foil. The foil rectangle is slightly larger. Use a pen to press down firmly and trace around the cardboard. Remove the cardboard. Now the metal foil is indented.

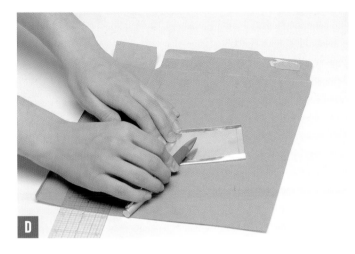

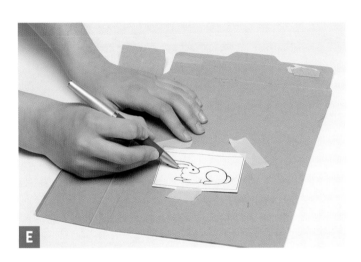

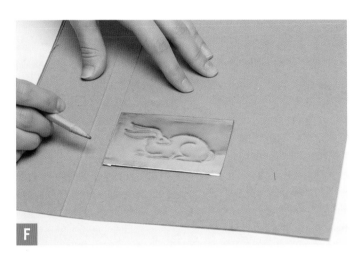

- Place a ruler along the top pen mark. Gently fold the edge of the metal up against the ruler. **C**

- Remove the ruler. Fold the bent strip all the way down. Smooth the fold by rolling the side of a pen or pencil over the crease. **D**

- Repeat the last two steps with the bottom pen mark, and then each side.

- Place the metal rectangle with its finished, folded edges on top of a notebook-size piece of leftover cardboard. The folded edges should be on the underside.

- Take the Repoussé Pendant Design bunny template. Cut out the rectangle.

- Place the paper image on top of the metal foil rectangle. They should be the same size.

- Use pieces of masking tape to hold down the edges of the paper and foil on the cardboard while you trace it. Then use a medium-point pen to carefully trace the outline of the animal. This will indent the design into the metal surface. **E**

- Peel up the tape and remove the paper. You should see an outline of the animal indented on the foil.

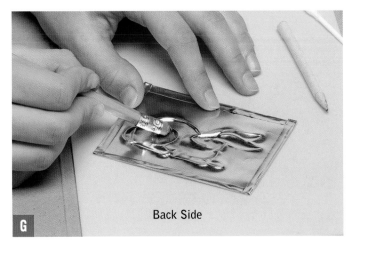

Back Side

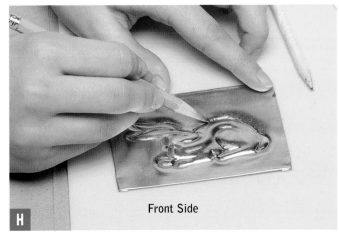

Front Side

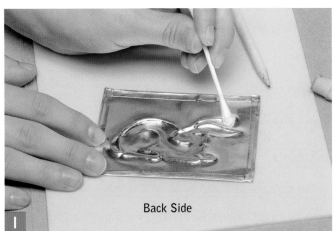

Back Side

- Trace around the animal again with the dull pencil. This will help define the lines. **F**

  ✔ **TIP:** If the pencil is too sharp, it could poke through the metal foil.

- Flip the metal foil over to the back side. Place it on top of the foam sheet. This surface will yield slightly, allowing the foil to be pushed out.

- Use the tip of the pencil eraser to gently press down on all areas of the design within the animal outline. Don't get too close to the outline or press on it! You are forming the embossed (or raised) area of the design now. **G**

- Flip the metal over again to the front side. Use the pencil to gently retrace the design outline. This will help emphasize the lines. **H**

- Flip the metal foil over again, so it is back side up. This time, use a cotton swab to press down on all the areas of the design within the outline. Now you can press closer to the outlines. **I**

- Turn the metal foil over to the front side. You should see the design popping out of the metal foil.

OPTIONAL PENDANT FEATURES

- Do you want to define the design's outline a bit more? Use the point of a pencil to lightly trace around the outline again. Or, trace around the design outline with fine-point permanent marker.

- You can also use paint or liquid shoe polish to define the outline. Take the paintbrush, cotton ball, or rag. Very gently brush or rub paint or shoe polish on the front side of the

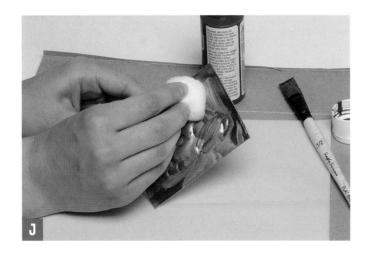

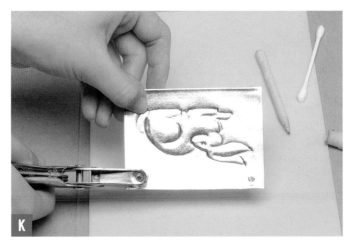

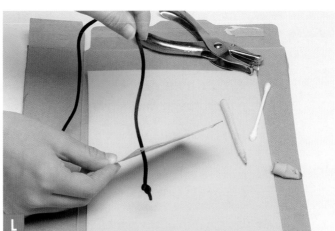

metal. Then lightly wipe it off before it dries. Be careful not to press too hard. Some of the paint or polish will settle into the lines. This will define it or give it more texture. **J**

STRING THE PENDANT

▥ Use the punch to punch two holes near the top edge of the pendant. **K**

▥ Take the string. Tie a knot at one end. Thread the string through one hole on the pendant, from the back to the front. The knot should be in the back of the pendant. **L**

▥ Place your beads on the string.

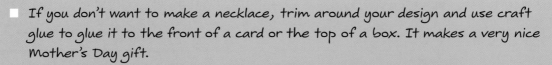

☐ If you don't want to make a necklace, trim around your design and use craft glue to glue it to the front of a card or the top of a box. It makes a very nice Mother's Day gift.

☐ Make up your own designs to emboss, or use the bird template we've included on page 178.

☐ Fill in the background of your foil design with dots or lines to add textures. Try varying how hard you press to see what that does.

■ Thread the other end of the string through the second hole in the pendant. Thread it from front to back. Tie a knot at the end of the string. The knot should sit behind the pendant. Distribute your beads so they are close to the foil.

You have created a beautiful necklace. Did you think this craft was easy or difficult? Can you imagine embroidering the same pattern in cloth with a needle and thread?

NIFTY '50s APRON

Skill Level 3

People have been wearing aprons for hundreds of years. Aprons have protected people's clothing from messy jobs throughout history. Without aprons, blacksmiths might be covered in soot. Butchers would get blood and guts on their clothes. Aprons protected carpenters and glass blowers from sawdust and hot glass. The clothes of cooks and artists have been saved by aprons. And the list goes on.

In the 1950s, people thought fancy aprons were essential for the woman of the house. Many aprons had ruffles and *rickrack,* which is a flat, zigzag trimming. Some housewives and mothers even wore their fancy aprons with pearls and high heels to serve dinner!

The Minnesota Historical Society has a collection of more than a hundred aprons. They date from the early 1900s to the 1980s. With this craft, you can create your own fancy apron. Yours will be a modern spin on a classic apron design.

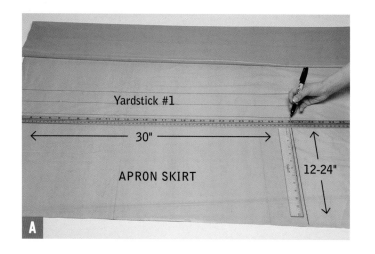
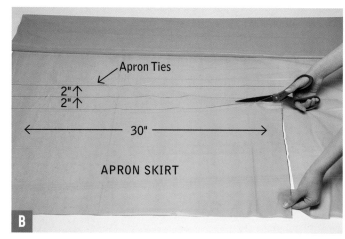

Supplies

- ☐ Plastic tablecloth (any color or pattern, 54 × 108 inches)
- ☐ Colored duct tape
- ☐ Decorative contact paper
- ☐ Several rolls of various colored tapes (could be duct tape, masking tape, or electrical tape)
- ☐ Scotch tape or painter's tape
- ☐ Hole punch
- ☐ Scissors
- ☐ Ruler
- ☐ 2 yardsticks
- ☐ Pen or permanent marker

Optional Supplies

- ☐ Sticky-backed foam shapes
- ☐ **Adult Help:** Hobby or craft knife and cutting mat

Directions

MARK THE APRON SKIRT AND TIES

- ▪ Lay the tablecloth out flat. You are going to draw a large rectangle and two long, skinny rectangles in the next few steps.

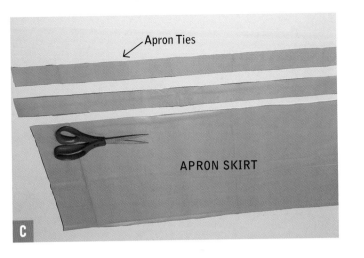

Apron Ties

APRON SKIRT

C

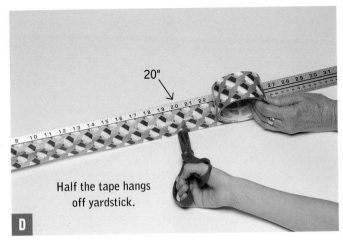

20"

Half the tape hangs
off yardstick.

D

- Decide how long you want your apron to be. It can be any length (12 to 24 inches). Use the yardstick to measure from your waist to your knee. Remember that measurement!

- From the bottom left edge of the plastic tablecloth, measure up that distance and make a mark. Repeat this on the right side.

- Lay yardstick (we'll call it #1) *horizontally* across the tablecloth at those marks and draw a line 30 inches long. A

- At the 30-inch mark, draw a *perpendicular* line straight down. This is the right side of your apron rectangle.

- Now you are going to draw two long, skinny *parallel* lines above the rectangle. These are the apron ties. On the left-hand side, measure up 2 inches from the top edge of the apron rectangle and make a mark. Repeat on the right-hand side.

- Lay the yardstick along those two marks and draw a line that is 30 inches long. Draw a second line 2 inches above the first apron tie. B

- Cut out the apron and apron ties along the marked lines. Set aside. C

PREPARE THE WAISTBAND

- Unroll and measure a piece of duct tape that is 20 inches long. Cut the duct tape and attach it to yardstick #1 lengthwise so half the width of the duct tape is hanging off the yardstick. D

  ✔ **TIP:** You might need some adult help for this step because the duct tape is sticky.

- You can lay the tape sticky side up away from your other material. Set aside yardstick #1 with the attached duct tape to use later.

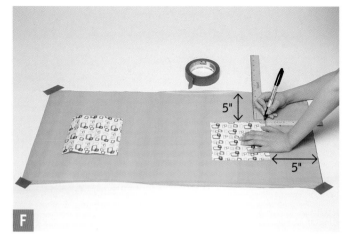

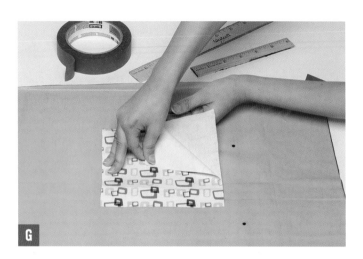

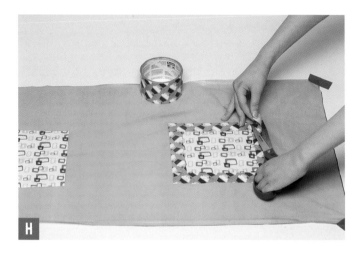

MAKE DECORATIVE POCKETS (OPTIONAL)

▧ Take the contact paper. Measure and mark two 6 × 6-inch squares on the contact paper. Cut the squares from the contact paper and then set aside. **E**

▧ Lay the cut rectangle of plastic tablecloth on a flat surface. This could be a table or the floor. Use a piece of Scotch tape or painter's tape on each corner of the plastic so it does not move.

▧ Take your ruler and one square of contact paper and position it 5 inches from the side of the apron and 5 inches down from top. Mark the position with a pen or marker. **F**

▧ Repeat this step with the other square of contact paper, positioning it 5 inches from the other side of the apron and 5 inches down from the top. Mark its position with a pen or marker.

▧ Peel off the backing of each square of the contact paper and place it where you made your marks for the pocket. **G**

▧ Cut pieces of duct tape that will make a decorative border on the top, bottom, and sides of the pockets. Use the tape to attach the pockets to the apron in the positions you marked. **H**

▧ If you like, make designs on your pockets with colored tape or stick-on foam shapes. **I** **J**

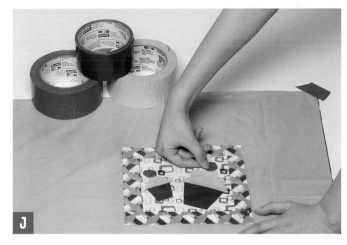

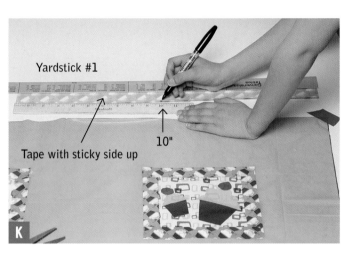

Yardstick #1

Tape with sticky side up

10"

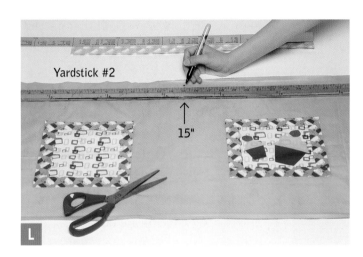

Yardstick #2

15"

✔ **TIP:** You can also create decorative shapes for your apron. Use scissors to cut shapes out of the duct tape or contact paper. Then stick them to the apron pockets.

Adult Help: You can also use a hobby or craft knife and cutting mat to cut shapes.

ATTACH THE WAISTBAND

▦ Take yardstick #1 that has the 20-inch piece of duct tape attached. It should still be lying flat, sticky side up on a table.

▦ Use a ruler to mark where the halfway point of the duct tape strip is. Don't place the ruler on top of the duct tape! It will get stuck. Lay it just below the tape. The center should be 10 inches from one end. Mark the center on the duct tape with a pen or marker. Be careful so your hand doesn't stick to the tape. K

▦ Move the long piece of duct tape that is still attached to yardstick #1 so it lays a bit above the tablecloth. It should run horizontal. Keep it sticky side up.

▦ On the top of the apron (where pockets are facing up) use yardstick #2 to measure the center of the tablecloth. The center will be at 15 inches. Make a mark with a pen or marker. L

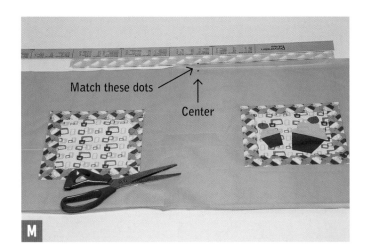

Match these dots

Center

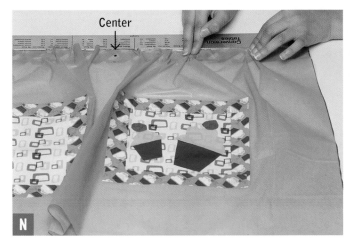

Center

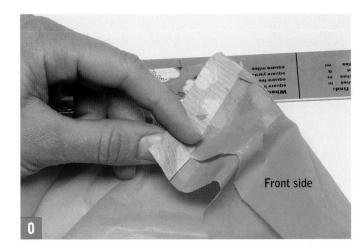

Front side

■ Remove the four pieces of tape that are holding down the tablecloth. Be careful it does not stick to the duct tape yet.

■ Carefully match up the mark on the center of the tablecloth with the mark that is on the center of the duct tape. Be careful that the tablecloth still does not stick to the duct tape. **M**

■ Holding onto the mark in the middle, pull the top edge of the tablecloth onto the bottom half of the duct tape so it bumps up along the edge of yardstick #1. Press down on the top center of the tablecloth so it sticks to the duct tape strip. Only the piece of tablecloth with the mark should be sticking to the tape. The rest of the top edge of the tablecloth should still be free.

MAKE PLEATS

■ Now you will make pleats. Use yardstick #1 as your guiding edge. To the right of the spot where the apron top is stuck on the duct tape, gather and pinch together the plastic a little. Press it down onto the bottom half of the duct tape. Make sure to keep the top edge of the tablecloth bumped up against the edge of yardstick #1. **N**

■ Continue to slightly gather, pinch, and then press the apron top edge onto the bottom half of the duct tape strip. Do this until you get to the last bit of apron on the right side.

■ Repeat the gathering, pinching, and pressing of the tablecloth onto the duct tape on the left side of the apron. The entire top length of the apron will be stuck to the tape.

■ Now it's time to peel off the duct tape from yardstick #1. There should still be 1 inch of duct tape sticking above the apron. **O**

■ Fold this 1-inch border of duct tape onto the front of the apron. It should cover the pinched parts of the plastic. Your apron waistband is almost done! **P**

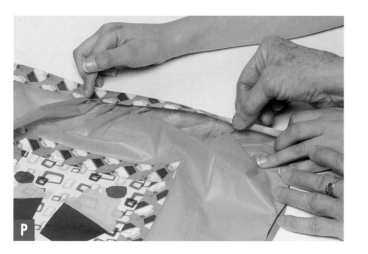

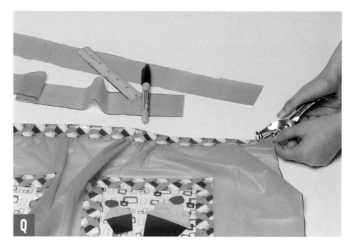

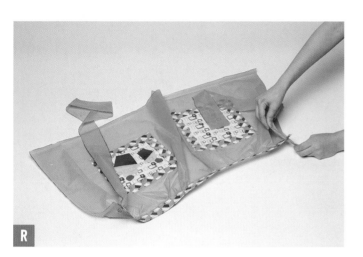

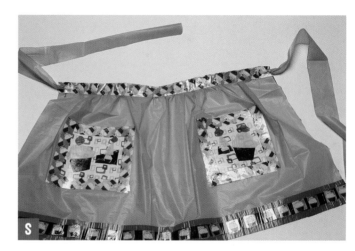

■ Cut another 20-inch-long piece of duct tape. Fold it over and cover the waistband with this second strip of duct tape to make it stronger.

MAKE APRON TIES

■ Line up the punch on one end of the duct tape waistband. Punch a hole about ½ inch in. Repeat at the other end of the waistband. **Q**

■ Grab the two long strips of plastic tablecloth you cut earlier. Thread one strip through the front to the back of one of the punched holes on the waistband. Tie it in a knot at the back. Cover the knot with a piece of duct tape on the back of the waistband. **R**

■ Repeat the step above with the other plastic strip on the other side of the waistband.

DECORATE THE HEM

■ Cut long pieces of the different colored tapes. Use them to add stripes or other designs to the bottom of your apron. **S**

Your apron is done. Wear it the next time you help in the kitchen. It can also protect your clothes as you work on other crafts in this book. Will you add pearls or high heels to your apron outfit like 1950s housewives did?

HMONG ROOSTER COMB HAT

Skill Level 1

I t's five o'clock in the morning, and it's already getting very warm and humid in a Hmong village in the mountains of Southeast Asia. A family sleeps with no alarm clock to wake them. But their rooster is a natural alarm clock. It wakes up the sleeping family with a loud, "*coo-coo-coo-coo-loo!*" Crowing at sunrise is part of the rooster's job as protector of the household.

Fast-forward 40 years. A Hmong brother and sister wake to the loud beep of an alarm clock. It's below zero outside. There is a ton of snow on the ground. The brother and sister live in St. Paul, Minnesota. Their family came from Laos. They left due to war in their country. Some Hmong people lived in refugee camps in Thailand from the 1970s to the 1990s. This family went to the United States to start a new life and settled in Minnesota, as did many Hmong people. The state now has one of the nation's largest Hmong populations. In fact, Minnesota's Twin Cities are known as the "capital of the Hmong world."

Many Hmong families weren't able to pack more than a few possessions when they left their homeland. But they did bring their traditions, one of which is a sewing technique of cross-stitch embroidery and appliqué. These important skills have been passed down through generations of Hmong women. They sew decoration on clothing for special occasions, such as the Hmong New Year. This holiday takes place over six weeks, from late November to early January. It is a time to celebrate and show off the best-decorated clothing Hmong women have made.

One traditional item is a rooster comb hat. The style was popular in the 1980s with Hmong girls and women from Laos who resettled in the United States after living in refugee camps in Thailand. It is made of bright colored fabric and has bold appliqué designs. Spikes and pom-poms at the top make the hat look like a rooster's comb. It is believed that the rooster, with a piece of the morning sky atop its head, still has symbolic and protective powers. In this craft, you'll make your very own protective and decorative Hmong rooster comb hat.

Supplies

- ☐ Hmong Rooster Comb Hat templates (pages 179–180 or at www.mnhspress .org/makinghistory), enlarged to 175 percent and printed on 11 × 17–inch card stock (see note page 8)

  ✔ **TIP:** Your home computer probably can't print out large sheets, so we suggest going to your local copy and print store to make the templates.

- ☐ Textile Stripe and Design Patterns templates (pages 181–182 or at www.mnhspress.org/makinghistory), 4 copies of each printed on white or colored 8½ × 11–inch printer paper

- ☐ Pom-poms in a variety of sizes and colors

- ☐ Variety of colored markers

- ☐ Glue stick

- ☐ ½–inch double-stick tape

- ☐ ½–inch double-stick foam tape

- ☐ Scissors

- ☐ **Adult Help:** Hot glue gun and hot melt glue

- ☐ Stapler and staples

- ☐ Staple remover

- ☐ Ruler or bone folder

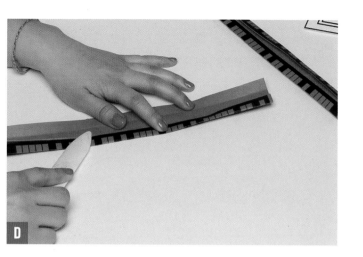

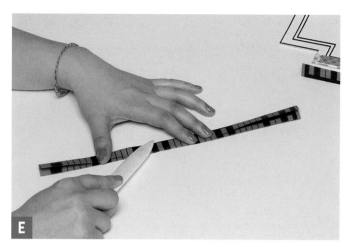

Optional Supplies

☐ Sticky-backed foam pieces in a variety of sizes and colors

☐ Clear packing tape

☐ Silver plumber's tape (found in hardware stores) or silver duct tape

☐ Colored 8½ × 11–inch printer paper

Directions

▣ Cut out the right and left sides of both Hmong Rooster Comb Hat templates. **A**

MAKE THE HAT TRIM

▣ Use the ruler to measure two 11-inch strips of double-stick foam tape. Cut the strips off the roll.

▣ Take one strip. Peel off one side of the protective layer to reveal the sticky part. Stick the tape along the outside bottom edge of one Hat Pattern cutout. Then peel off the protective layer facing up to reveal the tape's other sticky side. Set aside. **B**

▣ Repeat the step above with the second foam tape strip and second Hat Pattern cutout.

▣ Take one of the Textile Stripe Pattern sheets and cut out two matching patterns. These 2-inch-wide strips will be used to trim the bottom edge of the hat. **C**

▣ Take one strip and lay it flat, design side down. Fold both edges into the middle until they meet. Crease the folds lengthwise with the ruler or bone folder. The strip should look like a long strip with two little doors or shutters that meet in the middle. **D**

▣ Now fold the strip in half lengthwise one more time, so that the doors or shutters are sandwiched together on top of each other. Press on the fold and crease with the ruler or bone folder. **E**

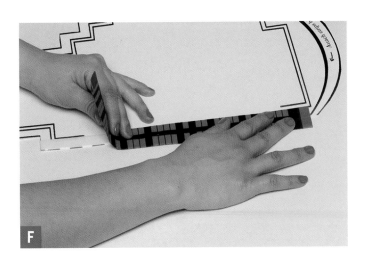

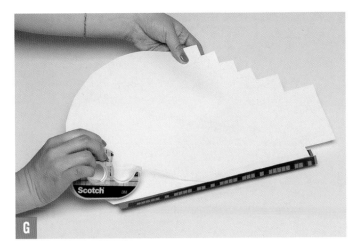

- Repeat the two steps above with the second Textile Stripe Pattern paper strip.

- Take one of the Hat Patterns you set aside. Take one of the folded strips. Place half of the inside of the strip on top of the sticky foam tape. Smooth down with your finger. **F**

- Repeat the step above with the other Hat Pattern and second paper strip.

- Turn each Hat Pattern over. Run a length of double-sided tape along the bottom edge. Fold over the other half

of the textile strip onto the tape. Press and smooth. You have created a headband on each Hat Pattern. **G** **H**

✔ **TIP:** If a bit of foam tape or paper strip is sticking out too far on either Hat Pattern, trim it off with scissors.

- Take another sheet of Textile Stripe Pattern and cut three matching strips lengthwise that are each about 2 inches wide. **I**

- Fold each strip's edge ½ inch into the middle. The three strips should look similar to the ones you just made, with long doors or shutters. Make creases and press them with a ruler or bone folder.

- Fold each strip lengthwise down the middle so the doors or shutters are on top of each other, like the other strips. Set aside the three paper strips. **J**

DECORATE THE HAT

- Cut up any size shapes and pieces of the leftover Textile Stripe Pattern sheets. Cut designs from the Textile Design Patterns, too.

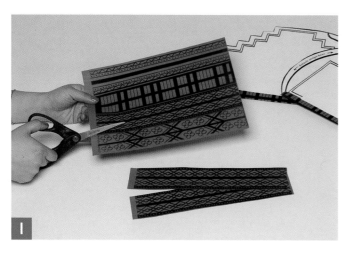

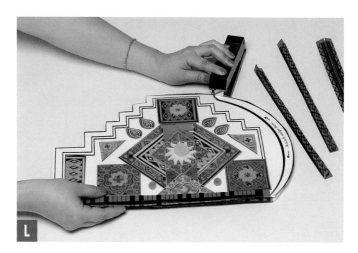

▦ Look at the photos on these pages to give you ideas. Cut out the shapes and lay them on the Hat Patterns before you glue them down. You can use double-stick tape to hold the pieces in place. Once you like your design, glue everything down with a glue stick. You can use clear packing tape to cover large sections. Did you gather the optional supplies of silver plumber's tape, markers, or sticky-backed foam shapes? Use them to decorate as well. K

✔ **TIP:** The designs on each side of your Hat Pattern don't have to match. Be creative and have fun!

▦ Take the two decorated Hat Patterns and place them together with the decorated sides facing out. Make sure the edges line up. Staple the top edge of the pieces together at one or two spots. L

▦ **Adult Help:** Staple the front of the hat that fits over your forehead. Now try the hat on your head and have someone help you adjust the back "tail" section so it feels comfortable. Use a pencil to mark the spot where you want the "tail" to be stapled, then remove the hat from your head and staple on the mark to hold the hat together. M (page 48)

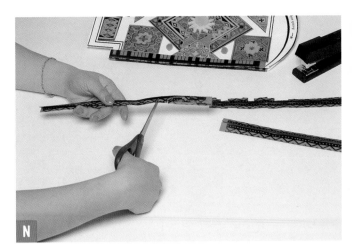

■ Your hat is almost done! Take one of the three folded paper strips you made earlier. Make small cuts on the *open* edge (*not* the center folded edge). This is to help you attach the strip to the curve of the hat. Sandwich the hat in between the folded strip, with one end even with the hat bottom or opening. Ease the paper onto the curve, making more cuts if needed so the paper fits. Staple the trim down. **N** **O**

■ **Adult Help:** Take the other two strips and once again make small cuts on the *open* edge. Have an adult help you run a thin line of hot glue along the curve of the hat, following the curved black line on the pattern. Attach a strip parallel to the stapled strip starting at the headband, and ease the paper so it bends. Cut the ends so they don't hang lower than the bottom of the hat. **P**

■ Repeat the step above with the other strip on the opposite side of the hat. When it is finished the curved piece looks fringed.

■ **Adult Help:** Finish your hat by hot gluing pom-poms on it. You can glue them anywhere you like for decoration. You can also glue them to the "comb" on top of the hat—it is the part that looks like stairs. **Q** **R**

Have fun wearing your Hmong rooster comb hat! Do you feel the rooster's protective powers? Wearing your hat might make you feel like practicing a rooster crow. You can also wear it as you learn more about Hmong culture and New Year.

MINNESOTA TRAPPER HAT

Skill Level 4

"**A**llouette, gentille alouette." Six paddles moved in perfect unison as the men sang. They propelled the huge canoe forward and continued singing, "Allouette, je t'y plumerai."

The year was 1780. This song and others like it rang out over the lakes and rivers of Minnesota as voyageurs paddled their birch-bark canoes. *Voyageur* is a French word that means "traveler." These travelers were heading to Fort Charlotte. They carried a cargo of furs to trade. They would transport their cargo and canoes overland, 8½ miles to Grand Portage, which is now part of the state of Minnesota.

The voyageurs were an essential link in the fur trading business in the 1700s and 1800s. They were French Canadians who transported goods for fur trading companies. It was a two-way exchange. Supplies and goods were dropped off, and beaver pelts, or hides, and other animal skins were picked up. These furs were valuable. They were traded and sold in European markets for use in clothing and hats. Top hats made from fur felt were popular at the time among wealthy men of Europe.

French Canadian traders, brought to far-flung communities by the voyageurs, set up posts where they exchanged goods with Native American men who trapped animals for the skins and for the meat. Some French Canadians married and raised families with Native American women. The Native American women who were married to fur traders also helped in the fur trading business. They interpreted for their husbands and provided important family connections to leaders and good hunters. Like other women in the community, they gathered wild rice, maple sugar, and many other foods that their families needed to eat. The fur trading companies provided Native Americans with valued manufactured goods as payment for furs. These included guns, metal cookware, and cloth. The partnership was beneficial for everyone.

In this craft, you will create your very own fur trader cap. It won't be made of real fur, though. Instead, you'll be *making* the fur! It will be made out of something you carry groceries in. Read on to find out how.

North Shore trapper, 1875

Voyageurs used birch-bark canoes to travel. The canoes were light and fast. They could also carry very heavy loads. Some could carry as much as 5 tons!

Supplies

- ☐ **Adult Help:** Trapper Hat Crown Section, Seam Line, Earflap, and Visor templates (pages 183–186 or at www.mnhspress.org/makinghistory), copied or printed on card stock (see note page 8)

- ☐ 3 paper grocery bags

- ☐ Heavyweight poster board

- ☐ Scissors

- ☐ See-through quilter's ruler (available at fabric stores and art supply stores; other rulers will work, but this one makes the job easier)

- ☐ Spring-loaded clothespins, paper clips, or other clamps

- ☐ Pen or pencil

- ☐ Stapler and staples

- ☐ **Adult Help:** Hot glue gun and hot melt glue

OVERVIEW OF TRAPPER HAT PIECES

You will make many pieces as a part of this craft. Below is a simple explanation of each piece.

- *4 crown sections.* These will be stapled together to form the crown. A crown is the top rounded part of a hat.

- *The band.* The band is the part of the hat that goes around your head. It supports all the other parts of the hat.

- *The visor.* The visor is the flap on the front of the hat.

- *The earflaps and straps.* This will be covered in paper cut to look like fur. It will be attached to the hat last.

OVERVIEW OF DIRECTIONS

This project has a lot of directions. The directions might look a bit complicated at first, but none of the steps are really hard. It is a good idea to have an adult help you so that it goes faster, though. It will also be helpful to read through these simple directions before you start your project. This way you will get an idea of the order of steps. Then you'll be ready to get started with the detailed directions that follow.

PREPARATION OVERVIEW

1. Copy or print templates on card stock and cut out. Trace template shapes onto grocery bags and cut out.

2. Cut band, mark quarters, and tape into a circle.

3. Cut the strip that covers the band.

4. Cut "fur" strips.

ASSEMBLY OVERVIEW

1. Staple crown sections together.

2. Attach crown to band.

3. Cover band.

4. Attach visor.

5. Mark fur attachment lines on earflaps.

6. Attach fur to earflaps.

7. Attach earflaps to band.

8. Attach straps.

9. Have fun wearing your hat!

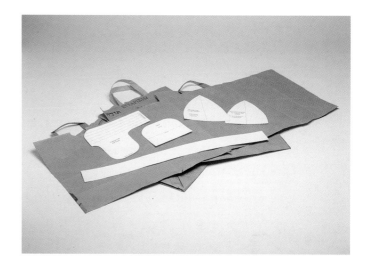

As they traveled, voyageurs often had to portage. This meant they had to carry their canoes over land in order to reach another lake or river. **Portage** is the French word for "carry." The town of Grand Portage, Minnesota, is named for a long portage of 8 1/2 miles.

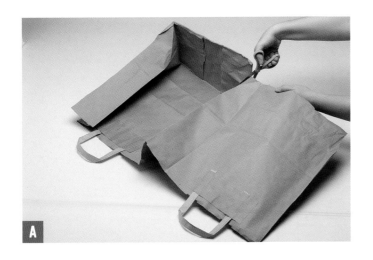

Directions

MAKE THE PATTERN PIECES

- Cut out all templates and set aside.

- Prepare the grocery bags. Take one bag and open it up. From the top, cut along one corner all the way to the bottom of the bag. Then cut the bottom off.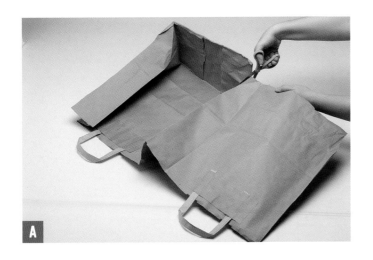

- Repeat the step above with one other bag. Now you have two big sheets of brown paper. Smooth them out.

- If there are handles on the bag, peel them off and set aside. Don't throw them away.

- Trace the Visor template onto the bag. Cut it out. Fold it along the fold line marked on the template.

- On an unprinted side of the bags, trace the Crown Section template four times. Cut them out.

- There are little marks shown on the Crown Section template. Transfer the marks to the bottom edge of the crown sections.

- Place the Seam Line template on top of a crown section. Line up the bottom of the template with the bottom of the paper bag crown section, between the two marks you just made. Trace around the template. Place a dot as shown at the top (apex) of the seam line template. Repeat this step for the other three sections. Set the four crown section cutouts and single visor cutout aside.

- Next, trace the Earflap. Fold the bag along one of its original fold lines. Place the marked fold line on your template along the fold of the bag. Use paper clips to hold the template while you trace. C

- When you cut the earflap, keep the bag folded. You will be cutting both sides of the paper bag at once. Don't cut the fold line, or you'll end up with two pieces instead of one!

   ✔ **TIP:** Use paper clips or clothespins to hold both sides together as you cut so that they are even.

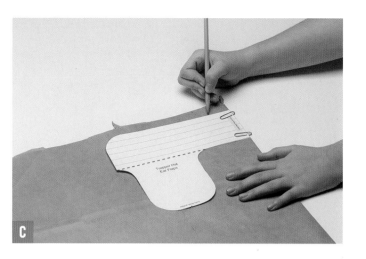

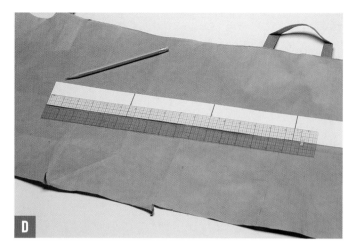

▥ Once the earflaps are cut out, set aside.

MAKE THE HAT BAND AND BAND COVERING

▥ On the poster board, measure and mark a long strip that is 2 × 22 inches. Cut the strip out.

▥ Starting at one end of your strip, place marks at these points:

5½ inches

11 inches

16½ inches

▥ Bend the strip into a circle with the marks you just made on the inside. Tape the ends together. Now you have a hat band. Set aside.

▥ To make the band covering, take one of the leftover pieces of paper bag. Measure and mark a strip that is 4 × 23 inches. Cut the strip out.

▥ After you cut that strip, fold it in half the long way. Set aside.

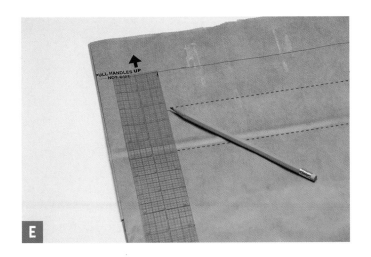

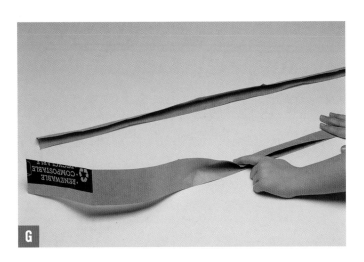

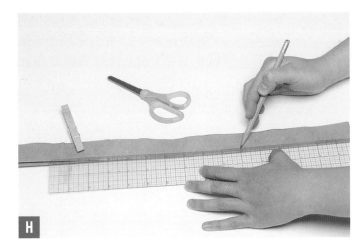

MAKE THE FUR STRIPS

▥ Lay an unopened bag on the table. You need to cut three 2½–inch strips. Starting at the top and moving down, measure and mark three parallel lines. The lines should be 2½ inches apart. Cut on the lines, cutting through all the layers at the same time.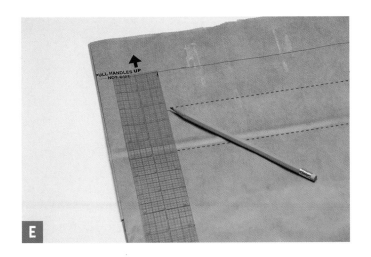

▥ Cut through each one of the strips so that it opens up into one long strip.

▥ Fold each of these strips in half lengthwise. They will be very long and skinny, like a belt.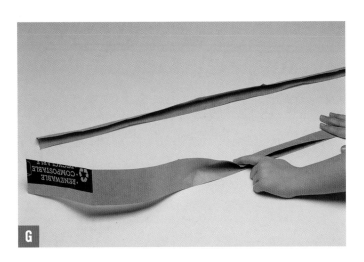

▥ Take each of the strips and fold them in half to make them shorter.

▥ Before you cut these strips into "fur" fringe, draw a "Stop! Don't cut past here!" line ¼ inch up from the folded edge. It's easy to do with a see-through ruler. Lay one strip on the table with the folded edge toward you. Lay your ruler on top of the strip. Move it down until you see only ¼ inch of it above the fold. Most of the ruler will hang off the edge onto the table. Press down hard on the ruler to keep it in place. Draw a line. Do the same thing to the other two strips.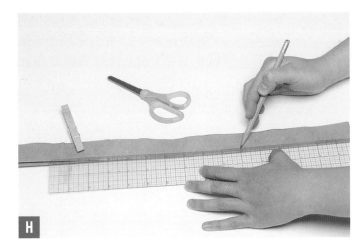

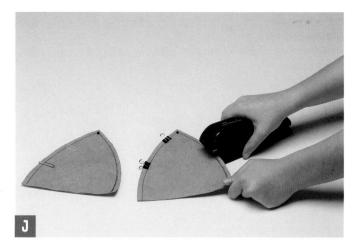

- Starting with the first strip, line up the folded edge of this doubled-up strip so the edges are even and right on top of each other. Paper clip or clamp the edges together so they don't wiggle around when you cut through them. Repeat with the other two strips.

- At the unfolded edge, make small vertical, or up and down, cuts into each strip. Make a cut about every ¼ inch or so. This will make the strip look like fringe. Don't worry if your cuts aren't very even or straight. Watch for the "Stop! Don't cut past here!" line to make sure you don't cut the strips into pieces. **I**

  ✔ **TIP:** You have to make a lot of cuts in this step! Ask someone to help you with this step so that it goes faster.

HAT ASSEMBLY

Now that all the pieces are cut and prepared, you get to put them together. This is the fun part!

ASSEMBLE THE CROWN

- Take two crown sections and lay them on top of each other. The seam lines that you drew earlier should be on the outside of both pieces, and the unmarked sides should be on the inside. Line them up evenly and clip them together. Staple the two pieces together along one edge on your seam line. Don't staple past the dot you marked earlier—and *just staple that one side*. Try to staple as close to the marked line as you can, but don't worry if the staples aren't *exactly* on the line. **J**

> The voyageurs were expected to work 14 to 16 hours a day. They were also expected to paddle 55 strokes per minute!

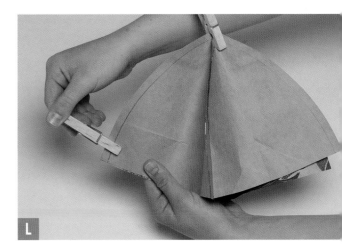

✔ **TIP:** In this next step, you will "finger press" the seam you just stapled. That's like ironing a seam to make it flat—only without the iron. This step will make the seam smoother so it will be easier to staple the two crown halves together later.

▦ Place one hand inside the stapled crown section close to the seam. With the other hand, gently press down on the seam in the same spot from the outside. Continue to do that for the whole seam. Set aside. **K**

▦ Take the other two crown sections and follow the same steps to staple them together and "finger press" the seams. You will end up with two half-circle double crown sections.

▦ Next, put the two halves together. Lay one double crown section on the table with the stapled side down. Take the other double crown section and place it on top with the stapled seam facing up. It's going to be a little tricky because they will not lay flat. Start by lining up the middle seams. Use a clothespin to clip them together. **L**

▦ Start at the left side and line up the two layers so they are even. Use a clothespin or paper clip to hold them at that left corner. (See L)

▦ Now do the same thing on the right side.

▦ In between those three clamps, clip the rest of the seam together and staple the two half circles together. **M**

▦ Finger press the seam. Now you have a full crown.

ATTACH THE HAT BAND TO THE CROWN

▦ Set the crown on the table. Ease the cardboard hat band you made earlier over the top of it. Push it down until it lines up with the bottom, open part of the crown that is resting on the table. **N**

▦ Pick up the crown and band and flip them over. Look inside the crown. Match each of the seam lines with the quarter marks that are on the inside of the hat band. Line up the bottom edges evenly. Tape the band and crown together at those four points. **O**

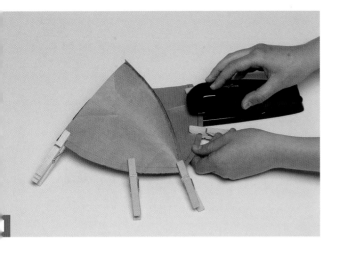

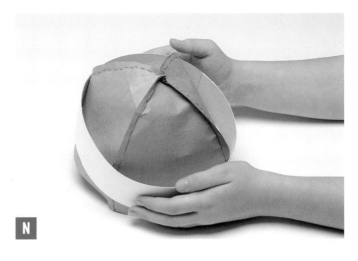

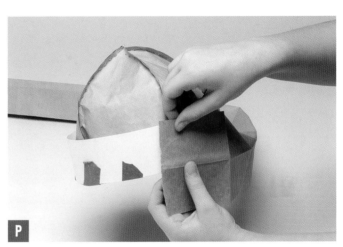

✔ **TIP:** Is the crown section a little too small, and won't reach the band? Release one of the staples at the bottom of one or two seams. This should allow the bottom to be opened a little wider. It's okay if there is a little gap. It won't show.

▦ Tape the middle of each of those four sections to the band.

✔ **TIP:** If the hat band is a little too big, make a little tuck (pleat) at the bottom of the crown section before you tape.

COVER THE HAT BAND AND ATTACH THE VISOR

▦ Take the band covering strip and line up the top edge of the strip with the top edge of the hat band. You can use a clamp to hold it while you use a glue stick to glue the strip around the outside of the band. The ends will overlap each other. **P**

▦ Fold the bottom half of the band cover to the inside of the hat and glue it in place.

▦ Position the visor between two seam lines, lining up the fold line with the bottom edge of the hat. The rounded half will be folded to the outside of the hat and the squared half will be glued inside the hat. **Q** (page 60)

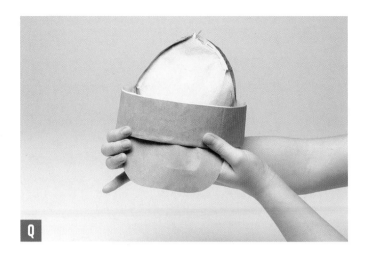

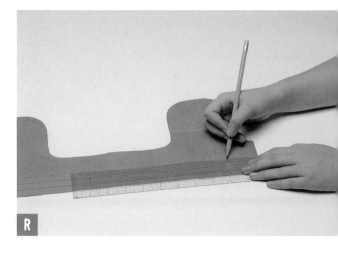

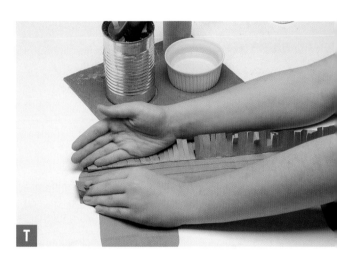

ATTACH FUR STRIPS TO THE EARFLAP

■ Mark five lines on the earflap with a ruler and pencil to match the template lines. They will start at the top and will be ½ inch apart. These lines will mark where you glue the fur strips.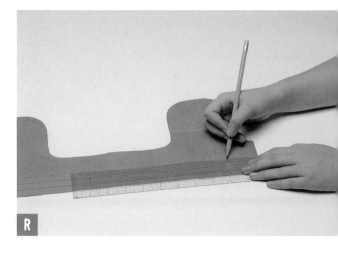

■ **Adult Help:** Have an adult help you run hot glue along about 3 inches of the top line. Stick the folded edge of one of the fur strips into the glue.

  ✔ **TIP:** When hot gluing the fur, continue to glue only about 3 inches at a time. The glue cools and hardens very quickly.

■ After one line is finished, push the fur toward the top edge so it's not in the way when you glue the next strip.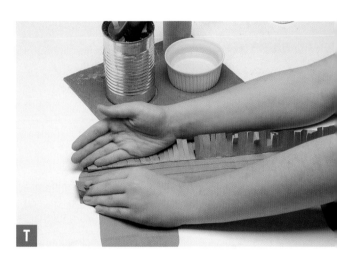

■ Continue hot gluing bit by bit until all five lines are glued with fur strips.

  ✔ **TIP:** It doesn't matter if you run out of fringe in the middle of the line. Just grab another piece and start gluing again. If the fringe is too long, rip it to make it fit.

■ Lay the fur-covered earflap on the table. Press down on the fur. This should crumple the paper a little to give it texture. U

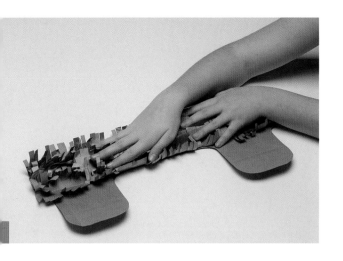

ATTACH THE EARFLAP TO THE HAT

- Center the earflap before you glue it to the hat. You're going to wrap the earflap around the hat, starting at one side of the visor and ending at the other side of the visor. Read on to find out how.

- There is a placement line marked on the Earflap template. Draw a line on the "unfurry" side of your earflap to match it.

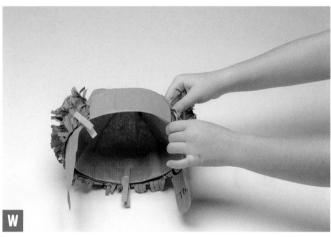

- Line up that line with the bottom edge of the hat, starting at one side of the visor. Use a clothespin to attach the earflap to the hat at that spot. **V**

- Wrap the earflap section around the back of the hat and attach it to the other side of the visor with another clothespin. Pay attention to the placement line while you do this. **W**

- Look at your hat. Do the sides look like they're an even distance from each side of the visor? If they are, you're ready to glue. If they aren't, you might have to move it around a little bit until they are.

- **Adult Help:** Once you have the earflap clipped in place where you want it, you are ready to glue it on. Remove the clothespin and glue one half of the earflap at a time. Start in the middle of the earflap, at the center back of the hat. Have an adult help you use the hot glue gun to attach.

- To complete your hat, glue or tape chin straps to the inside of the bottom middle of the flaps, as shown on the template. If your paper bags had handles, use them here as straps. Otherwise, cut a scrap of paper to make two straps. The ones we used were each ¾ × 15 inches.

Enjoy wearing your hat. Imagine if it were made out of fur, like the voyageurs' hats. It would be a lot heavier, but a lot warmer!

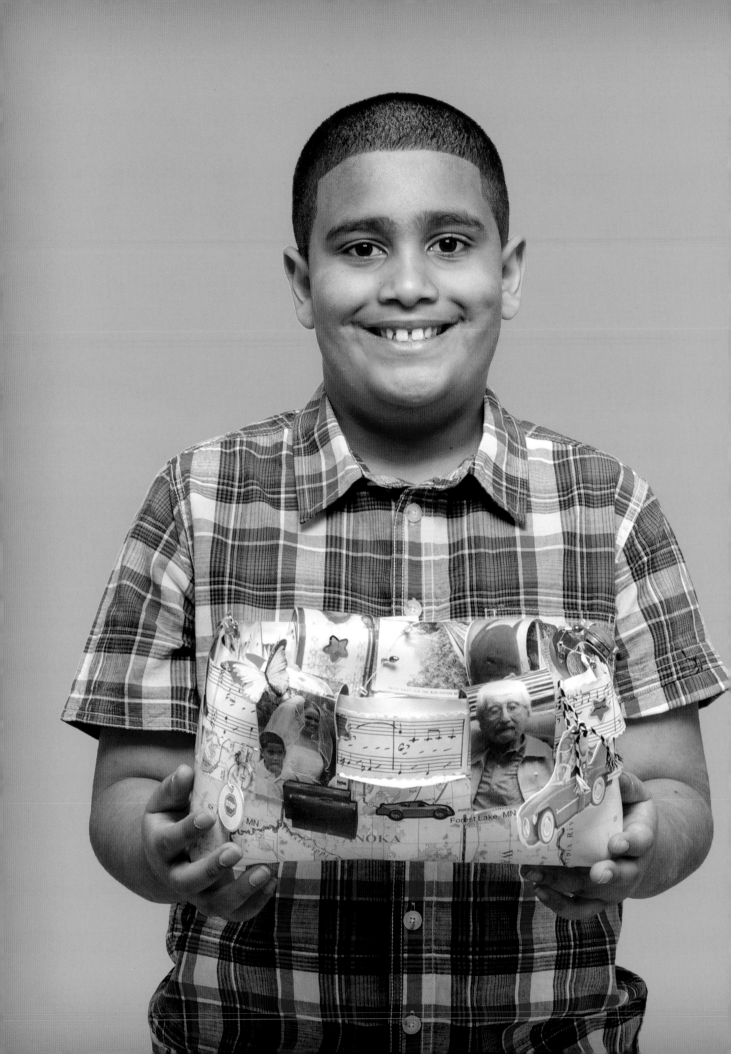

MAKAK GENERATION BASKET

Skill Level 3

A makak (*mah-кинк*) is a container made of white birch bark. It is used for cooking and for hauling water. It is also used to gather berries and wild rice, and to store maple sugar and other foods. It keeps food fungus-free and ready to eat.

Birch-bark containers

Makak baskets have a clever one-piece design. They are laced together using bark fibers or other plant materials. Ojibwe (*oh-jib-way*) people began creating makaks long ago. The Ojibwe migrated from the East Coast in the 1600s. They settled along the Great Lakes in what is now Minnesota and Wisconsin. As they journeyed west, they made use of the land's plentiful resources. The four seasons guided their lives and living arrangements. They set up winter and summer villages to hunt and fish. They harvested wild rice in the fall. In the spring, the Ojibwe turned sap from maple trees into sugar.

Because there are numerous modern containers for cooking and storing food, the Ojibwe people no longer need to make makaks. But many Ojibwe people still carry on the

Ojibwe women winnowing rice using makaks, early 1900s

tradition of working with birch bark to create artwork. Some even put a new spin on the art. Pat Kruse and his son Gage live in the Lake Mille Lacs area of Minnesota. Pat has worked with birch bark since he was eight years old. He learned techniques from his mother. Pat and Gage can make just about anything from birch bark, including traditional baskets, containers, and even hats! They

63

Pat and Gage Kruse

My Brother's Blanket #3, by Pat and Gage Kruse,
38 × 36 inches

also like experimenting with the material, so they work together to create "birch bark paintings." Pat designs the compositions. Gage sews together all of the birch bark pieces with deer sinew. "I'm like the composer," explains Pat, "and my son is like the band. I write the music, and he plays it."

In this craft, you will put your own spin on a traditional Ojibwe art form by making a makak generation basket inspired by the pattern of the birch-bark makaks. It is also inspired by another Ojibwe tradition: oral storytelling. The basket will be made out of a map of your city, state, or other important location. Then you will use family photos, favorite trinkets, and other mementos to decorate the basket. Weave memories onto the basket using photocopies from special occasions, such as a vacation, birthday, or family holiday. The basket will display the story of your life.

Supplies

- ☐ Large travel map of somewhere special (your city, state, or a vacation location)

- ☐ Photocopies of family photos (any size, black and white or color)

- ☐ Photocopies of mementos, such as sheet music, recipe cards, seed packets, poems, drawings, postcards, fabric pieces, sports event or movie tickets

- ☐ 1 roll of clear contact paper

- ☐ Variety of scrapbooking paper or decorative paper

- ☐ Stickers

- ☐ Charms, trinkets, and other small items (buttons, pom-poms, beads, small toys)

- ☐ Flattened, stiff cardboard (cereal box or poster board)

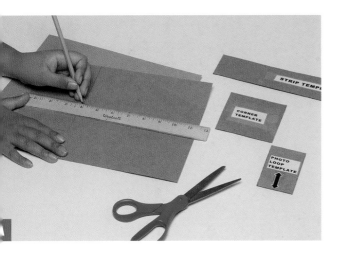

- ☐ Scissors
- ☐ Hole punch
- ☐ String
- ☐ Ruler
- ☐ Yardstick
- ☐ Stapler and staples
- ☐ Staple remover

- ☐ Glue stick
- ☐ Scotch tape
- ☐ Pencil
- ☐ Dark-colored permanent marker
- ☐ Paper clips
- ☐ **Adult Help:** Hot glue gun and hot melt glue
- ☐ Ruler or bone folder

Directions

PREPARE PHOTOS

▦ **Adult Help:** Go through photo albums or scrapbooks and choose 12 images. Make copies of each. You can take them to a store with copy services. Or you can scan and print them on the computer if you have a scanner, computer, and printer access.

MAKE TEMPLATES FOR TRACING

▦ Measure and mark a square on the cardboard that is 3½ × 3½ inches.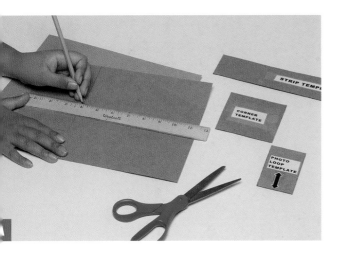

▦ Cut out the square. Write "CORNER TEMPLATE" on it with marker.

▦ Measure and mark a strip on the cardboard that is 2 × 11 inches.

▦ Cut out the cardboard strip. Write "STRIP TEMPLATE" on it with marker.

▦ Measure and mark a rectangle on the cardboard that is 2 × 3½ inches.

▦ Cut out the rectangle. Write "PHOTO LOOP TEMPLATE" on it.

▦ Set all templates aside.

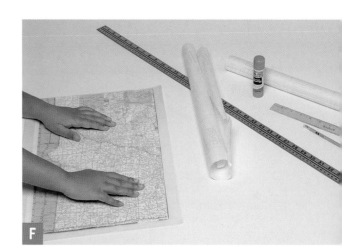

MAKE THE BASKET BASE

▤ Take the travel map and fold in half. Cut the map in two.

▤ Measure the pieces. Trim each piece as needed so each is 11 × 17 inches. **C** **D**

▤ Roll out some clear contact paper. Lay one map piece on it. Roll enough out so that the contact paper is a little bigger than the map. Cut the contact paper. Then cut another piece of contact paper that is the same size. Set aside.

▤ Take the two map pieces. Glue them together with the glue stick. Make sure the map sides you want showing are facing out on each side. **E**

▤ Take one piece of contact paper. Peel off the backing. Lay the contact paper flat with the sticky side up.

▤ Lay the double-sided map in the center of the sticky contact paper. There should be a bit of contact paper sticking out on all sides. Smooth the map onto the paper.

▤ Take the second sheet of contact paper. Peel off the backing.

▤ Carefully lay the contact paper sticky side down on top of the other side of the map. The maps should now be sandwiched between contact paper. **F**

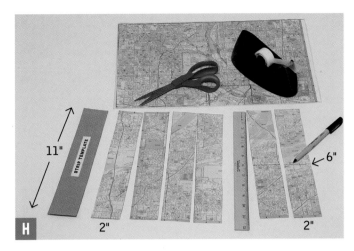

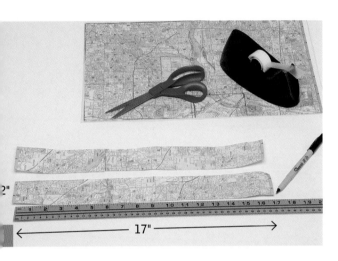

- Smooth the contact paper so there are no bubbles.

- Trim the edges of the contact paper on all sides of the map. Set covered map aside.

MAKE THE BASKET RIM

- Take the STRIP TEMPLATE and your decorative or scrapbook paper. Or, if you have a lot of map left over from trimming, you can use that instead.

- Trace the STRIP TEMPLATE onto the paper six times. Cut out the six strips. **G**

- Set four of the strips aside. Take the other two and use the ruler to measure and mark the strips at 6 inches. **H**

- Cut the strips at the 6-inch marks. Keep the 6-inch pieces. Toss what you cut off.

- Take one 6-inch-long strip and tape it to the end of one of the 2 × 11–inch strips. This will make one extra-long strip that is 2 × 17 inches. **I**

- Repeat the step above with the second 6-inch-long strip and another 2 × 11–inch strip.

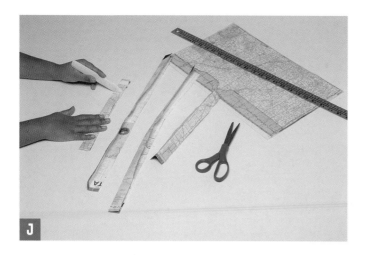

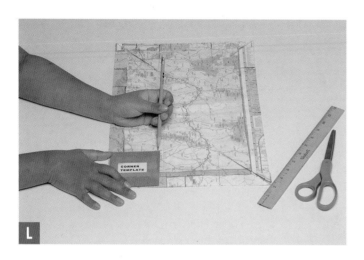

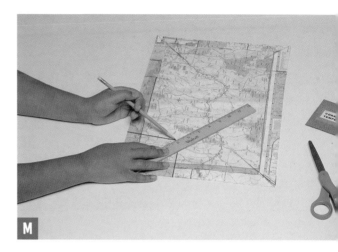

- You should now have four strips total:
  Two that are 2 × 17 inches
  Two that are 2 × 11 inches

- Fold and crease each strip in half along its length. Use the bone folder to press on the crease.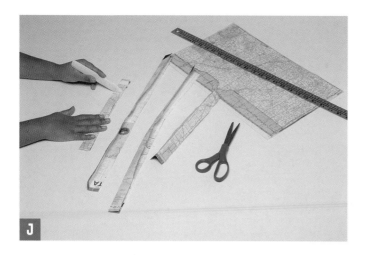

- Place the map in front of you on the table. Place each long strip just above a long side of the map. Place each short strip just above each short side of the map.

- Next, you will sandwich the map edges inside the creased strips. Open one of the longer folded strips so it is somewhat flat again. Spread glue on the inside of the strip with the glue stick.

- Glue the strip to a long side of the map. Fold the strip over the map edge. Half the strip will be glued on the back of the map. The other half should be glued onto the front of the map. The map edge should line up with the crease. Smooth the strip so it is flat.

- Repeat the last two steps with the other folded strips:
  Glue the other long strip over the edge of the other long side of the map.
  Glue the two shorter folded strips over the two shorter sides of the map.

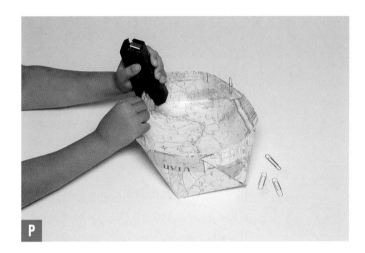

The rim on your basket is done!

FOLD THE BASKET

- Take the CORNER TEMPLATE. Use a pencil to trace the shape in each corner of the map. L

- Draw a diagonal line from each map corner to the opposite corner of the traced square. M

- Cut the diagonal lines. N

- At the cuts in each corner, take up one flap. Pull it behind the flap it touches. Each should overlap and pull that corner of the map up, to make a basket shape. Use paper clips to hold the corner pieces in place. O

- Repeat the step above on the other side of the map. The map should now look like a basket.

- When you are happy with the shape, staple each side of the basket where the flaps overlap. You will need to use at least two staples to hold the flaps in place. Then remove the paper clips. P

MAKE THE PHOTO LOOPS

▦ Take the PHOTO LOOP TEMPLATE and one copied photo. Place the template over the part of the photo you want on your basket. The shorter sides of the template are the top and bottom. Make sure you place the template over the photo to match this direction. Trace the template onto the photo with the permanent marker. Cut out the photo or image. Q R

▦ Repeat the step above to make a total of 12 photo cutouts.

▦ Group the 12 photo cutouts into pairs.

▦ Take one photo pair. Lay the images flat so the top of each image is touching. (One image will be upside down.) Use Scotch tape to attach the pair together at the top. This should make the two photos into a strip that, when folded in half at the tape, has a photo on each side. S

▦ Repeat the step above with all other photo pairs. You will end up with six short photo strips. These will be the loops on the basket.

▦ Now you're going to make a backing for the photos. Cut six decorative paper strips that are each 2 × 7 inches.

▦ Take one taped-together photo pair. Flip it over so the images are facing down. Place one decorative paper strip on the photo backs so the edges line up. Glue the paper onto the back side of the photo pair. T

▦ Repeat the step above with the other photo pairs and paper strips.

▦ Take one photo strip with paper backing. Use paper clips to attach it to the rim of the basket in a loop. The paper backing should be on the inside of the loop. The photos should be on the outside of the loop. U

▦ Repeat the step with all photo strips. Space them out along the basket rim as you like.

▦ **Adult Help:** Once the loops are where you like, you are ready to attach them for good. Remove the paper clips from one loop. Have an adult help you place a line of hot glue at the bottom edge of one end of the loop. Glue that loop end to the *outside* rim of the

basket. Place another line of hot glue on the other end of the loop. Glue that end to the *inside* rim of the basket. (See U)

- Repeat the last step with all six photo strips. Set basket aside.

WEAVE THE STRIPS

- Take the STRIP TEMPLATE. Take the decorative paper, or your photocopies of sheet music, postcards, or any other paper you gathered. Trace the template end to end on the paper to make a long strip. Make the strip as long as you can on one piece of paper. Cut the strip out. Trace and cut another long strip, as long as you can make it. Tape the long strips together and use a yardstick to measure their length. Cut and tape together more strips until you have one long strip that is 2 × 34 inches. **V**

- Repeat the step above to make another 2 × 34–inch strip.

- Use a glue stick to glue the two strips together back to back to make one double-sided strip.

- Take the double-sided strip and carefully weave it through the photo loops on your basket. Do this until the entire strip is woven through. Trim one end if it is too long, then tape the ends of the strips together. **W** (page 72)

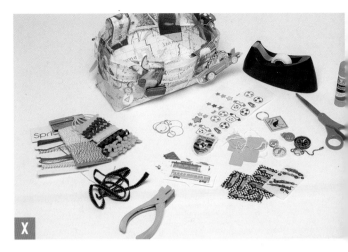

ADD FUN FEATURES

Your basket is almost done. Now is the really fun part: adding more decorations!

- **Adult Help:** Take the trinkets, charms, toys, or decorations you gathered. Attach them to the basket wherever you like. Have an adult help you use hot glue to attach them. You can also add stickers, buttons, beads, or anything else you like. Use a punch to make holes in some photos. Then punch a hole in any tickets or paper decorations you like. Tie them onto the photo with string. X

Your makak generation basket is complete. Take a minute to look it over. There are a lot of memories on it. Think about the people, places, and things you used and why they're special to you. Use your basket however you like. Maybe it will hold more mementos as you save them up to make another basket!

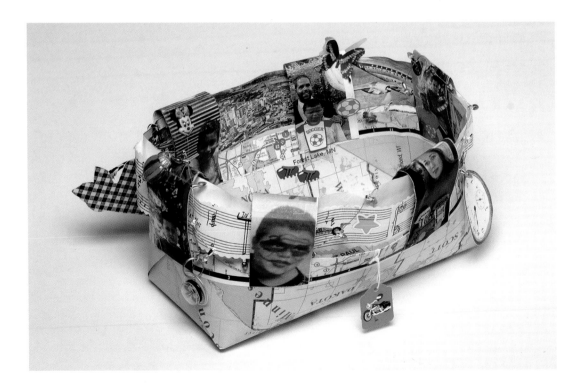

CIVIL WAR SEWING KIT

Skill Level 2

I t was 1861. Lieutenant Wilford C. Wilson was a soldier with the 11th Minnesota Infantry Regiment, Company B. That year, he marched off with his unit to fight in the Civil War (1861–1865). Before he left, Wilson's sweetheart gave him a special gift: a sewing kit called a "housewife." The housewife was small and lightweight. It could be rolled up and stuffed inside the heavy haversack the soldier carried on his back with his gear. The kit was durable, too. This one has survived for 150 years. Today it is part of the Civil War artifacts collection at the Minnesota Historical Society.

Inside the kit are two pockets made of leather and silk. There is also a needle keeper, thread, sewing needles, and straight pins. The kit is bound with cloth tape. It has a wide ribbon used to tie it closed. Lieutenant Wilson no doubt appreciated this thoughtful gift. He and the other men in his unit were given only one wool uniform, which had to last them through their entire service during the war. The tools in the kit would be useful for sewing tears and holes and replacing buttons. It was also a loving reminder of the home he was fighting for.

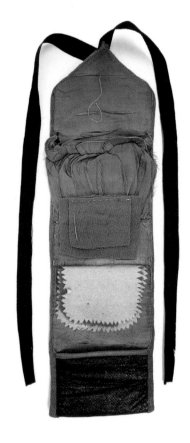

The Civil War was not fought on Minnesota soil, but it had a great impact on the state and its people. Minnesota was part of the Union, led by President Abraham Lincoln. It was the first state to respond to Lincoln's request for volunteer armies to defend the Union against the Confederacy. The war was fought over several issues, including slavery. The Confederate states wanted slavery to continue, and the Union states fought to end it.

Minnesota sent 25,000 men into the war. This was about half of the state's male population that was old enough to serve at the time. Most of the Minnesota soldiers who fought were white men, but more than 100 black men and many Native Americans from Minnesota also served.

The war ended in April 1865, when the Confederate states surrendered. The nation was reunited, and slavery was abolished.

The Minnesota Historical Society has a large collection of Civil War artifacts. These include government records and manuscripts, books, and diaries. There are also photographs and art from that time. Visit www.mnhs.org to learn more about Minnesota and the Civil War.

In this craft, you will make your own housewife sewing kit. It will hold all sorts of useful things. You might give it away as a gift, as Lieutenant Wilson's sweetheart did. Or you might use it to hold small supplies for your sewing projects.

This is a regimental battle flag of the 11th Minnesota Infantry, used in the Civil War. It is one of many artifacts from the war in the Minnesota Historical Society's collections.

Supplies

- ☐ Calico fabric (approximately ½ yard)
- ☐ 2 sheets felt
- ☐ Ribbon
- ☐ Needles
- ☐ Thread
- ☐ Safety pins (variety of sizes)
- ☐ Straight pins
- ☐ Buttons (variety of sizes and colors)
- ☐ Scissors (and/or pinking shears)
- ☐ Duct tape (any color)
- ☐ Glue stick
- ☐ Ruler
- ☐ Pen
- ☐ Small spool of thread with a hole in the middle of the spool (often found in travel-size sewing kits)

Optional Supplies

- ☐ Decorative trims (lace, bows, embroidered decals, old jewelry)
- ☐ Needle threader

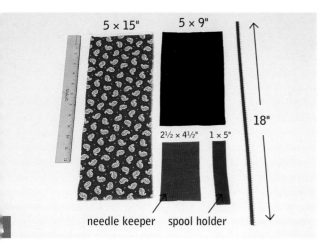

5 × 15" 5 × 9"

2½ × 4½" 1 × 5"

18"

needle keeper spool holder

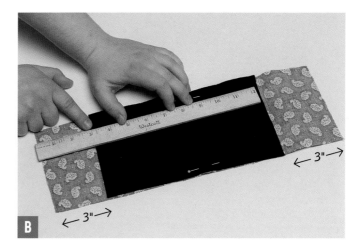

← 3" → ← 3" →

B

☐ Miniature sewing scissors

☐ Embroidery appliqués

Directions

PREPARE THE PIECES

▦ Use a ruler to measure a rectangle of calico fabric that is 5 × 15 inches. Mark the measurements with a pen. Cut out the rectangle and set aside.

▦ Measure and mark a rectangle on the felt that is 5 × 9 inches. Cut out the rectangle and set aside.

▦ Measure and mark a rectangle on the felt that is 2½ × 4½ inches long. Cut out and set aside.

▦ Measure and mark a felt strip that is 1 × 5 inches. Cut out and set aside.

▦ Measure and cut a piece of ribbon that is 18 inches long. Set aside. **A**

▦ **Adult Help:** Take the calico rectangle. Flip it over and lay it flat so the printed side of the fabric is facing down. Place the felt rectangle on top of the calico, in the center. Leave 3 inches of calico fabric sticking out on either side of the felt. Use a few straight pins to hold the felt in place. **B**

MAKE THE POCKETS

▦ **Adult Help:** Fold about ¼ inch of the calico fabric at one end toward the felt. Press down on the fold with your finger to crease it, and then pin it in place. **C**

▦ Repeat the step above on the other end of the calico fabric.

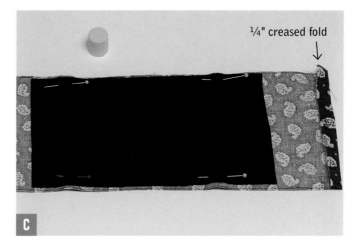

¼" creased fold

C

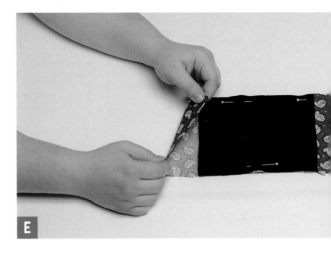

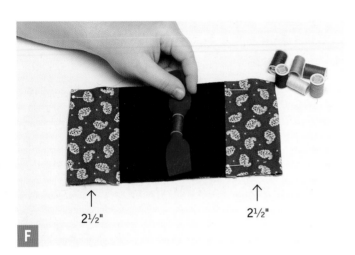

- Use the glue stick to glue the ¼-inch fold down onto the back of the calico.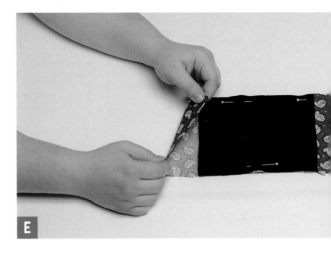

- Repeat the last step at the other end of the calico fabric.

- **Adult Help:** Take one end of the calico. Fold it into the center of the felt rectangle, 2½ inches on each side. Have an adult help you pin the calico down to hold it in place.

- Repeat the last step with the other side of the calico fabric. These are the pockets!

MAKE THE SPOOL HOLDER

- Take the small felt strip you cut earlier. Lay it vertically across the center of the rectangle.

- Grab the small spool of thread. Thread the felt through the hole in the spool. Slide the spool onto the middle of the felt strip.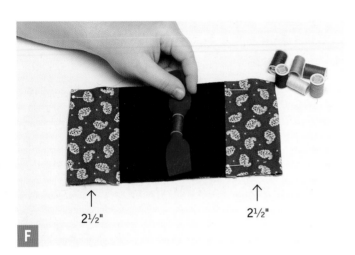

- **Adult Help:** Have an adult help you use straight pins to hold the felt strip in place.

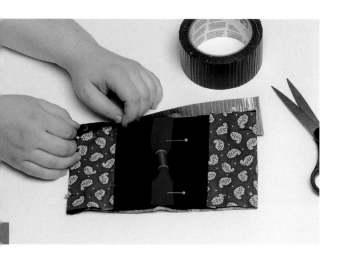

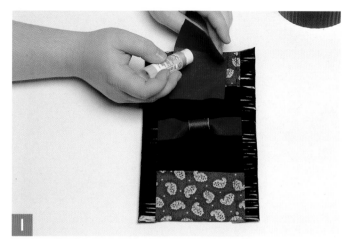

BIND THE KIT

▦ Take the duct tape. Cut a piece that is about 10 inches long.

▦ Fold the duct tape lengthwise on the long edge of the felt and calico. Half the tape should be on the back side. The other half should run along the length in the front. If any tape hangs off the end, trim with the scissors.

▦ Repeat the last two steps on the other long side of the felt and calico.

▦ Remove all straight pins.

MAKE THE NEEDLE KEEPER

▦ Take the 2½ × 4½–inch piece of felt you cut earlier and lay it down so the long sides are on the left and right.

▦ Measure and mark 2¼ inches from the top side. Fold the felt on that line. (The bottom layer will stick out a bit farther than the top layer.)

▦ Place the folded felt at one end of the calico rectangle. Line up the felt fold with the calico fold. Spread glue from the glue stick underneath the bottom of the felt piece. Glue it to the calico fabric.

▦ Place a bit of glue in the fold of the felt. Press the top layer down onto the bottom layer. Press on the felt fold with your finger. This step will glue the top layer of felt to the bottom at the fold.

▦ Optional: Trim edges of felt with pinking shears. (page 80)

▦ Measure and cut a strip of duct tape that is 6 inches long.

▦ Fold the duct tape lengthwise over the short edge of the calico and the fold of the felt needle keeper. Half the tape should be on the back side. The other half should be on the front. If any tape hangs off the end, trim with the scissors.

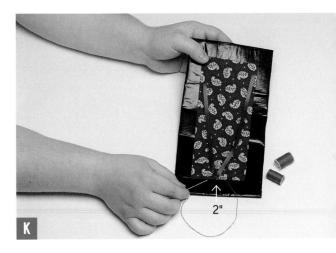

- Measure and cut another 6-inch strip of duct tape.

- Cover the remaining short edge of the calico with the duct tape. Trim tape with scissors.

- Remove all pins.

ADD THE TIE CLOSURE

- Flip the entire project over. The spool holder and needle keeper should be facing down, on the table.

- **Adult Help:** Use the ruler to measure 2 inches in toward the center from one short end of the calico. Have an adult help you mark the spot with a straight pin.

  ✔ **TIP:** This spot should be on the opposite end of the needle keeper and right above the duct tape border.

- **Adult Help:** Have an adult help you prepare a needle and thread. Set aside.

- Take the ribbon. Fold it in half.

- **Adult Help:** Have an adult help you stitch the fold of the ribbon to the outside of the calico where the pin is. **K**

- Remove the pin.

ADD SUPPLIES AND DECORATION

- **Adult Help:** Your housewife kit is almost done. Flip the entire thing back over so that the pockets, needle keeper, and spool holder are facing up. Poke safety pins through the calico pockets. Have adult help you hang closed safety pins from them.

- **Adult Help:** Secure another safety pin on a pocket and have an adult help you thread buttons on

- **Adult Help:** Have an adult help you stick needles in the needle keeper.

- If you gathered mini sewing scissors or a needle threader, place them in the calico pockets. You can also sew on buttons, embroidered appliqués, or personal items, such as a locket or jewelry.

- Add items to the pockets, too. You can keep whatever you like in them. Extra buttons and thread are good things to store here.

- Roll up your sewing kit starting at one short side. Then tie the ribbon around it to keep it closed.

Your sewing kit is complete. Will you give it away as a gift? To whom? Or will you keep it for yourself? It could hold the thread, felt pieces, and safety pins you need to make another sewing kit as a gift!

"GONE FISHING" ICE HOUSE

Skill Level 3

T all tales and fishing have hung out in the same boat together for a long time. In fact, exaggerated descriptions of the "fish that got away" are called *fish tales*. These stories are often so incredible that people don't know if they are true. And if you spend some time in a Minnesota ice house—fishing through a hole in the ice—you're likely to hear a tale or two. Maybe even one like this:

It was January 1888. A fellow named Sven Stevenson was sitting in his outhouse at the top of a hill. An outhouse is an outdoor bathroom, because there were no indoor bathrooms in those days! A shack and a toilet seat over a hole. That's all there was.

It had been a long, wet fall. The rain ran in rivers that cut through the soil, and it weakened the hillside. As Sven sat in his outhouse, he suddenly felt the ground begin to move. And then it slid. Sven, the outhouse, and a big chunk of icy dirt slid down the snowy hill—right onto the frozen Lake Minnewaska! They say that the friction of the dirt sliding across the ice created enough heat to melt a hole through the ice.

Fish Houses, Cameron Booth, 1923

When the outhouse came to a stop, Sven looked down through the hole in the outhouse floor. It was lined up right over the hole in the ice! He could hardly believe his eyes. Fish were swimming around! So what did Sven do? What any good angler would. He ran back to his cabin, grabbed his fishing rod, and returned to his outhouse to fish.

It wasn't long before Sven's friends sacrificed their own outhouses to set on the lake. They wanted to ice fish from inside a shack, too! And that, it is said, is how ice houses were born. Is this fish tale fact or fiction? No one will ever know. When the ice melted that spring, Sven's ice house sank, never to be seen again.

Though ice houses are somewhat new in terms of history, people have been ice fishing for hundreds of years. Before Europeans immigrated and settled in Minnesota, Ojibwe and

Dakota people got food during winter by fishing through holes they chopped in the ice. A fisherman built a small framework of sticks and covered them with a blanket. Then he lay face down on the ice, his head and shoulders under the blanket. With the sunlight blocked, he could see clearly to a great depth. The fisherman then lowered a wooden lure attached to a stick into the hole. Holding a three-pronged spear in the other hand, he jiggled the lure to make it "swim," and when an unsuspecting fish swam up to grab the lure, *ziiiing!* A quick stab. Fish for dinner!

Inside an ice house, 1953

With long winters and more than 10,000 lakes, Minnesota is still a popular place for ice fishing today. However, changes have occurred over time. Now anglers pull their houses onto the ice with trucks and snowmobiles. They drill holes with gas-powered ice augers. They locate fish with GPS devices and sonar fish finders. And they relax with their friends in heater-warmed houses. Some ice houses even have beds and televisions!

One thing hasn't changed, though. The rule about removing the houses before ice-out remains the same—and for a good reason. Ice melts and houses sink.

You won't have to worry about your ice house sinking come spring, though. You'll make a miniature version of an ice house that can be kept indoors! Use it for play—or to store memories from a fish tale of your very own.

Supplies

- ☐ **Adult Help:** Stovepipe, Stovepipe Backing, Roof, Front Roof Support, Back Roof Support, Front Wall, Back Wall, and Floor templates (pages 187–188 or at www.mnhspress.org /makinghistory), copied or printed on card stock (see note page 8)

- ☐ **Adult Help:** Hot glue gun and hot melt glue

- ☐ Glue stick or craft glue

- ☐ 10 popsicle sticks

- ☐ Scissors

- ☐ Scotch tape

- ☐ ¼–inch hole punch

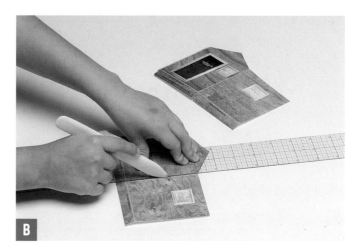

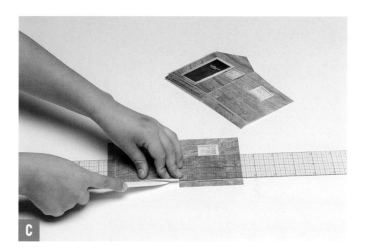

- ☐ Ruler

- ☐ Flexible plastic straw

- ☐ Pencil

- ☐ Newspaper to cover your work space

- ☐ Black permanent marker (washable markers won't stick to the plastic straw)

- ☐ Butter knife or bone folder

- ☐ Small piece of corrugated cardboard

Directions

PREPARE THE PIECES

- Cut out all printouts, but make sure you *do not* cut the gray and gold lines. They are fold lines! Set the Stovepipe and the Stovepipe Backing aside. **A**

SCORE THE FOLD LINES

- Take the cut printouts and lay them flat on the table with the printed side up. Next, score the fold lines. You will indent the line in order to make it easier to fold. Take one of the pieces. Line up the ruler on one of the fold lines. Use your bone folder or butter knife to press down along the line to indent it. **B**

- Keep the ruler in position on the fold line. Slip the bone folder or butter knife under the paper. From the underside, use your tool to press the paper up toward the ruler. Press it against the ruler all along that edge. This step will bend the paper exactly on the fold line and make it easier to fold there later. **C**

- Repeat the last two steps on all fold lines of all printouts.

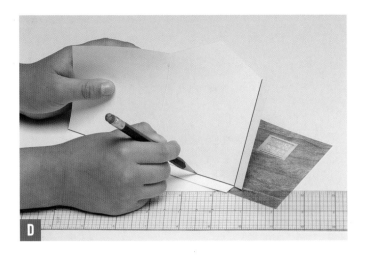

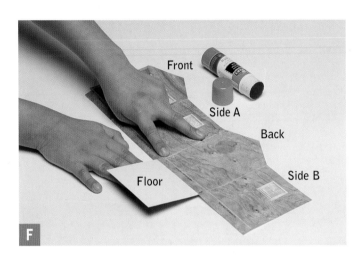

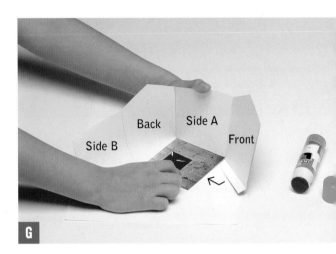

■ Gently re-fold the score lines of each of your pieces in the opposite direction. Press down along the fold with the tip of your finger. Flip the printout over so the unprinted, or blank side, is facing up. Use a pencil to trace a line along each of the creases you made. **D**

GLUE THE HOUSE AND FLOOR TOGETHER

■ Next, put these pieces together to make a box without a lid. The box bottom will be a floor. You can even see fish swimming!

■ Take the Back Wall piece. Lay it so the printed side is facing down. The back peak (the top of a roof, like the point of a triangle) is pointing away from you.

■ Take the Floor piece. Hold it so the floorboards run up and down and the fish are closer to the flap. Use a glue stick to glue the right-hand flap. Lay the Floor so the edge is snug up against the fold line of the flap. Press the Floor firmly against the flap to hold. **E**

■ Flip over this Back Wall/Floor piece so that you see the printed side of the wall. Now the side with the floor attached will be on the left-hand side.

CONSTRUCTION DIAGRAM

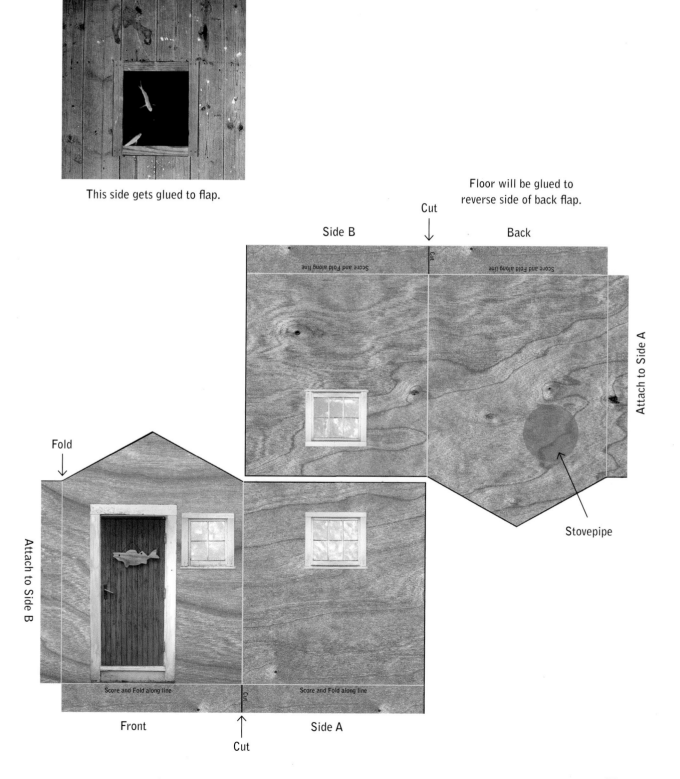

This side gets glued to flap.

Floor will be glued to
reverse side of back flap.

Cut

Side B

Back

Score and Fold along line

Score and Fold along line

Attach to Side A

Fold

Stovepipe

Attach to Side B

Score and Fold along line

Score and Fold along line

Front

Side A

Cut

Cut

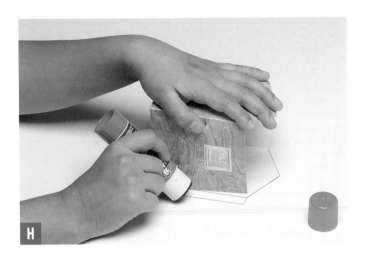

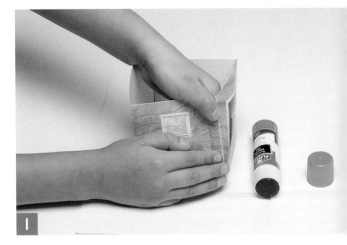

Take the Front Wall. Lay it down so that you can see the front door. In the next step, you will glue the Front and Back Wall sections together.

✔ **TIP:** Pay attention to the horizontal printed line that runs along the top of all four flaps. Make sure that line matches and is straight across.

Use a glue stick to glue the vertical flap on the left-hand side of the Back. Lay Side A on top of the glued flap. Smooth the edge of the wall with your finger to make sure the pieces are glued together securely. **F** (page 86)

Stand the house up, with the Floor to the inside. **G** (page 86)

✔ **TIP:** You may need to re-fold the flaps so the house can stand up. You will see the fish and the unprinted side of the walls. The bottom flaps are bent to the inside. In the next steps you will turn this into a box.

Glue the flap on Side A that is to the right side of the Floor. Bend the wall so that you can place the Floor onto it, snug up against the wall.

Repeat this step with the other two walls and flaps so that the Floor is glued all the way around. The vertical corner will still be open.

Lay the house on its side. The unglued flap should face up so that you see the unprinted side. Glue it and then press it onto the outside of the house. That closes the corner. Press the corner from the inside at the same time you press the outside to secure. **H** **I**

GLUE ON THE POPSICLE STICKS

Take the ruler and six popsicle sticks. At each end of one stick, measure ⅝ inch in. Mark the lines with a pencil. Use this stick as a guide to mark the other five sticks in the same way. These lines will help you center the house on the sticks. **J**

✔ **TIP:** You are going to glue these six sticks into a square shape on the bottom of the house. They will run along the outside edge. They will alternate, so read the directions carefully.

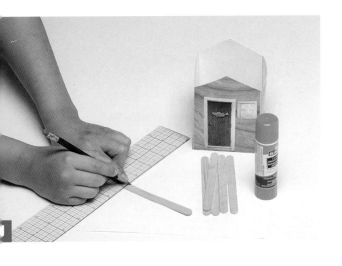

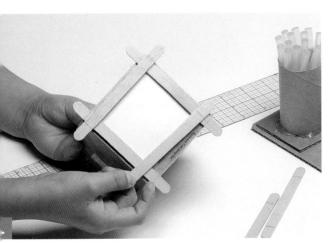

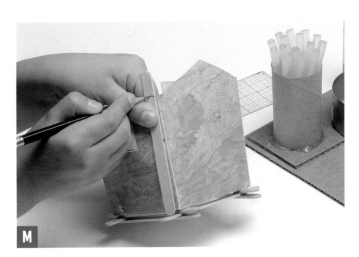

■ **Adult Help:** Place one stick onto the bottom of the house along the outside edge, running from front to back. Center the house between the marks you drew. Hot glue a line along that edge and immediately press the stick into the glue. Repeat with a second stick, running it from front to back along the opposite edge. **K**

■ **Adult Help:** Next, glue two more sticks in the same way, but from side to side. **L**

■ **Adult Help:** Glue the last two sticks you marked. They will match the first two and run from front to back.

■ Take the four popsicle sticks that you have left. Line up one stick at the vertical corner of the side wall. (*Sticks will be glued on the sides, not the front or back of the house.*) The rounded bottom of your stick should touch the top of the stick you glued to the bottom. Make a mark across the top of your vertical stick to match the top edge of the house. Use a scissors to cut the popsicle stick at the line. Ask for help if it's hard for you to cut through the stick. **M**

■ Use the cut popsicle stick to measure and mark a line on the three other popsicle sticks. Cut them to the same length.

■ **Adult Help:** Hot glue one cut popsicle stick straight up and down to a vertical corner of the house.

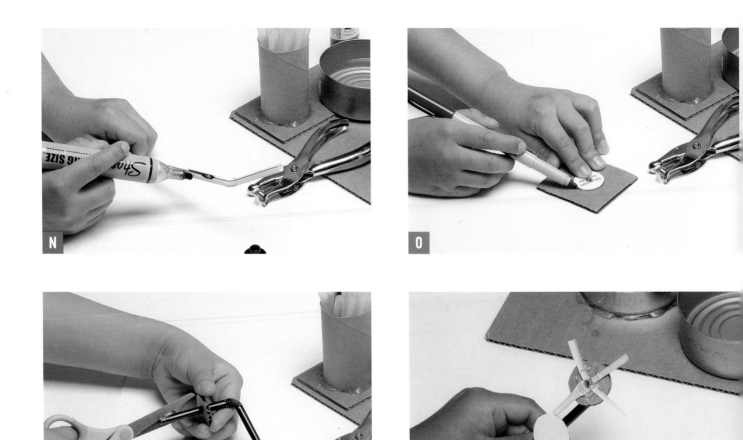

■ Repeat the last step with the last three popsicle sticks on all vertical corners.

PREPARE THE STOVEPIPE

■ Take the straw and the marker. Hold the straw at the end that doesn't have the flexible joint. Use the marker to color the rest of the straw, including the joint. You don't have to color the end that you are holding. Let it dry. **N**

■ Once the straw is dry, measure and cut the part you just colored to be 4½ inches long. Set aside. You don't need the leftover piece of straw.

■ Take the Stovepipe template. Punch a hole in the middle where it's marked.

■ Trace the Stovepipe template on the corrugated cardboard and cut it out. Punch a hole in the cardboard to match the hole in the template. **O**

■ Take the straw. Bend the joint so it looks like an elbow. Poke the shorter end through the cardboard until ½ inch shows on the other side. Insert one blade of the scissors into the ½-inch piece and clip in until you reach the cardboard. Make three more cuts like this to create four flaps on the end of the straw. **P**

■ Push the cardboard circle back toward the elbow. Bend each of the flaps out and pinch

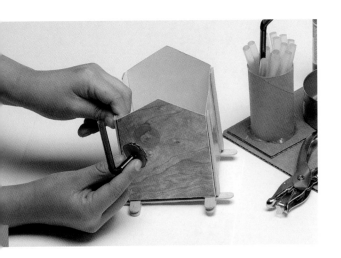 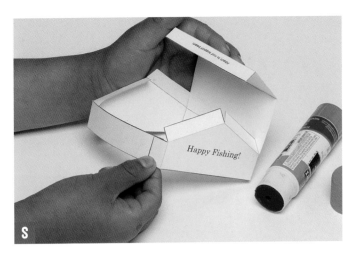

them so they have a sharp crease. Push the cardboard back down, snug against those creases. The flaps may stick out past the cardboard.

- Next you will sandwich the straw flaps between the cardboard and the Stovepipe Backing. Your fingers will be underneath.

- **Adult Help:** Put a circle of hot glue on top of the fanned straw and cardboard. Put the Stovepipe Backing on top and press down. **Q**

- Trim straw pieces if any of them stick out past the edge.

- **Adult Help:** Take the ice house and find the circle on the back side. Put a dab of glue on the circle and quickly press the stovepipe onto it. **R**

PREPARE THE ROOF SUPPORT

- Look at the two Roof Support cutouts. Take the Front Roof Support that says "Happy Fishing." When you put it together with the Back Roof Support, it will look like a box without the bottom.

- Line up the two parts so that the sides with the peaks face each other. Fold the two small flaps on each peak to the inside of the box. They will support the roof. **S**

- Each of the peaked sections has a flap on the left side. You will glue the sections together with those flaps. Use the glue stick to glue them together at the corners. Glue the flaps to the outside. (See S)

- Fold the "box top" over the peaked ends—but first glue the top of the support flaps that are folded to the inside. Lay the box top onto the flaps. Tuck the remaining flap to the inside, like you're tucking in the flap of a box top. You can tape it in place on the inside. **T U** (page 93)

ATTACH THE ROOF TO THE ROOF SUPPORT

- Lay the Roof on the table, unprinted side up. The pencil line you marked earlier on the crease should run down the middle. Line up the V-shaped edge of the top (the Roof

CONSTRUCTION DIAGRAM

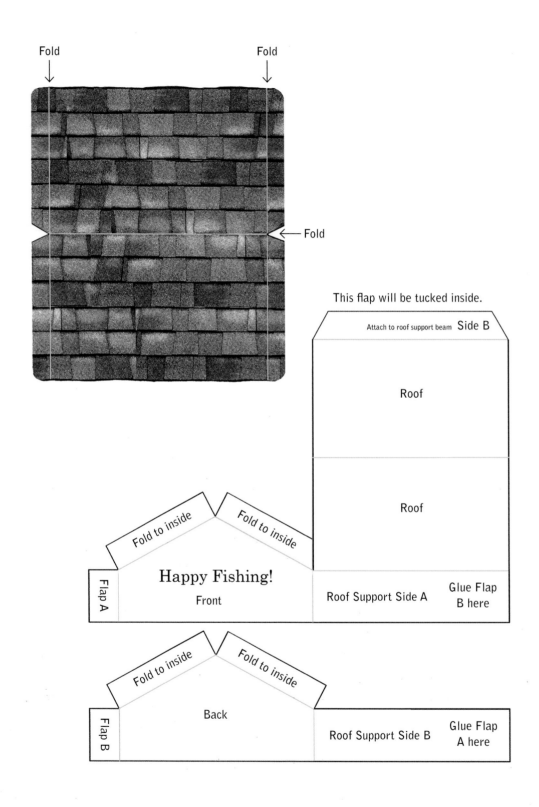

Fold

Fold

Fold

This flap will be tucked inside.

Attach to roof support beam Side B

Roof

Roof

Fold to inside

Fold to inside

Happy Fishing!

Front

Flap A

Roof Support Side A

Glue Flap
B here

Fold to inside

Fold to inside

Back

Flap B

Roof Support Side B

Glue Flap
A here

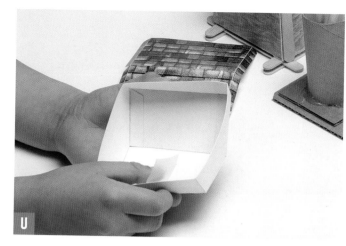

Glue here

Support) along that line. Center it so that it is equal distance from the front and back edges.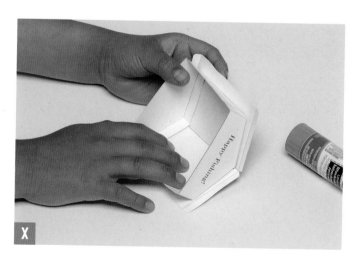

▦ Use a glue stick to add glue to half of the Roof. Roll the top of the Roof Support over onto the glue. Press down to make sure the pieces stick together. **W**

▦ Repeat the last step with the other half of the Roof and the Roof Support. Flip the box over. Now you have a real roof. **X**

Set the roof onto the house with the words "Happy Fishing" in the front. It should sit on top of the house like a lid. It will not be glued. That way you'll be able to take the roof off and see inside the house.

Your ice house is complete. Make your own ice village and fish for goldfish crackers. Or use it like a real box and give it to your favorite angler to hold lures. Happy fishing!

BURNING SPEAR STORY STAFF

Skill Level 2

Maurice Carlton was a junk genius! He loved recycling things. He would transform broken toys, magazine clippings, stickers, old lumber, photos, and other random stuff into such creations as weather vanes, neighborhood shrines, crowns, and headdresses. He also made telescopes that he said could see into the future. Why did Maurice make these things?

Maurice was a retired train engineer. He volunteered for St. Paul's Inner City Youth League in the 1960s and 1970s. He would walk around the neighborhood wearing his handmade clothing and unique hats, and he also carried a special walking stick. Maurice called the stick Burning Spear. He decorated it with photos, written sayings, and maps. The carved staffs used by court advisors of African kings were what inspired Maurice to make his Burning Spear. These advisors were respected public speakers and storytellers. The staffs represented their power to speak.

Maurice used his staff as a tool for starting conversations. People would ask him about the stick, and this would start a conversation about the staff decorations and what they meant. In this craft, you will make your own burning spear story staff. What items will you use to decorate it? What conversations do you think it will start? You will be a storyteller with your staff, just like those African advisors in kingdoms far away.

Maurice Carlton portrait, 1976

Maurice Carlton made many art creations in his lifetime. Sixteen of them are in the Minnesota Historical Society's collections. They include hats, spears, and signs for the Inner City Youth League.

Can you guess what materials Maurice used to make the hat pictured here?

This wide-brimmed, boater-style hat is made from many materials. The top is made from a red vinyl phonograph record. The brim of the hat is made from a black vinyl record. The sides are made of black cardboard. On top of the hat is a paper disk with a black-and-white photograph. The photo shows Maurice wearing one of his hat creations. There is also a photo of the Inner City Youth League building. The sides of the hat have black-and-white photographs of children playing musical instruments.

Supplies

- ☐ Sheet of poster board (any color)

- ☐ Colored duct tape

- ☐ Clear packing tape

- ☐ Several small items (anything from this list: trinkets, old toys, jewelry, holiday ornaments, buttons)

- ☐ Heavy corrugated cardboard

- ☐ Glue stick

- ☐ **Adult Help:** Hot glue gun and hot melt glue

- ☐ **Adult Help:** Gorilla Glue

- ☐ Scissors

- ☐ Marker

- ☐ Yardstick

- ☐ Stapler and staples

- ☐ A few plastic lids in various sizes (plastic food container lids work well)

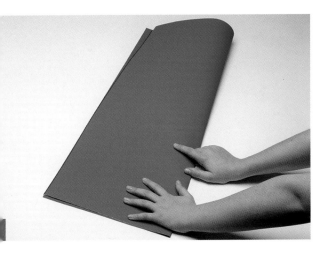

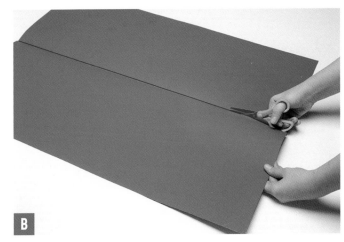

Optional Supplies

- ☐ Pieces of fabric or decorative paper
- ☐ Paint
- ☐ Colored masking tape
- ☐ Wrapping paper
- ☐ Contact paper
- ☐ Stickers
- ☐ Fake fur trim, lace trim, or holiday garland
- ☐ String or ribbon
- ☐ Aluminum foil
- ☐ Maps, printed poems, photos, and/or magazines

Directions

MAKE THE STAFF

▦ Fold the poster board in half lengthwise. Open it up again. Cut in half on the crease. You will have two long rectangle pieces. **A** **B**

▦ Place one rectangle above the other so that one short side from each rectangle is touching.

▦ Take the yardstick. Pull one rectangle down on top of the other until the entire length of the overlapped rectangles is about 38 inches. This will be how tall your staff is.

✔ **TIP:** If the 38-inch-long rectangle seems too long or too short, you can pull the top piece up or down to make it longer or shorter.

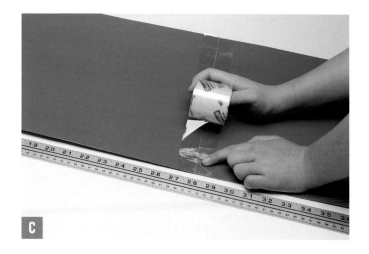

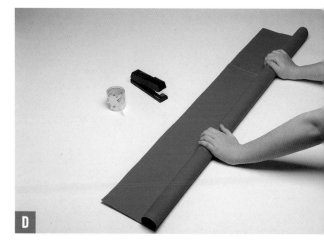

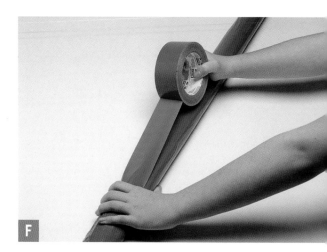

- Make sure the long sides of the rectangles are lined up where they overlap. Once they are, tape the two pieces together on the front and sides with packing tape. Flip over and tape the back overlap together, too. You should now have one very long, thin rectangle. **C**

- Tightly roll up the poster board lengthwise to make a tube. Wrap packing tape around the middle of the tube. This should keep the tube together. **D**

- Staple the overlapping poster board together at each tube end. Place half the stapler inside the tube to do this. Make sure you do not staple the tube closed at the ends!

- Wrap several pieces of packing tape around the tube. Space them out. **E**

- **Adult Help:** Cut a long piece of duct tape. It should be almost as long as the tube. Cover the tube lengthwise with the strip of duct tape. Have an adult help you place the tape. It can get tricky! **F**

  ✔ **TIP:** It's okay if the duct tape is wrinkly. The wrinkles will add interesting texture to your staff.

- Cut and place more long lengths of tape until the tube is completely covered in duct tape.

MAKE THE FINIAL BASE

The *finial* is what will go on the top of your staff. It can be anything! It might be an old toy. It could be a trinket or old piece of jewelry, too. Select an object from your gathered items that represents something about you or is something you really like. It should be something that can start a conversation and tell a story. The finial will sit on a base that will get glued to the top of the staff. **G**

> ✔ **TIP:** Having trouble thinking how an item will start a conversation? People might ask you what the finial represents. A toy car, boat, or airplane finial could represent a family road trip. An animal finial might represent a visit to the zoo.

▓ Choose one of your gathered items that you want to use as the finial piece.

▓ Place your finial piece on the heavy cardboard so it is standing up. Take a marker and draw around the base of the item. It's okay if the outline is not perfect. **H**

▓ Take the plastic lids. Place them over the outline you just traced. See which one is the right size to cover all of the traced marks. You should not see any markings when you place the lid over the outline. **I**

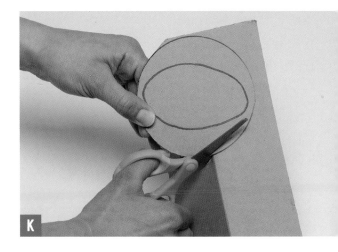

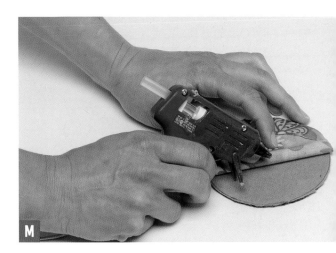

▦ Once you find a lid that covers the outline, trace around it on the cardboard with the marker. **J**

▦ Cut the traced circle out of the cardboard. Have an adult help you cut if the cardboard is too thick. **K**

▦ Next, decorate the cardboard circle. What you use will depend on what you gathered. If you have paint, you can paint it. If you have fabric, decorative paper, or contact paper, you can trace the circle onto them and then cut out the traced pattern. **L**

▦ **Adult Help:** Use a hot glue gun to attach fabric or paper, or pull off the backing of the contact paper and cover the top of the cardboard base. **M**

▦ **Adult Help:** When the base is decorated, it is time to attach the finial. Have an adult help you hot glue the finial on the top of the base.

✔ **TIP:** Gorilla Glue works great to attach plastic toys to a surface. Make sure to read the directions on the back of the bottle.

▦ **Adult Help:** You can also have an adult help you hot glue any garland or trim around the cardboard circle's edge. **N**

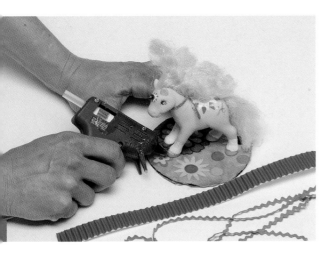

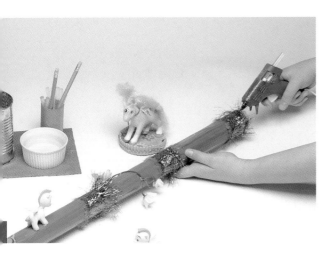

> *Something new from something old.*
> *Something good for the soul.*
> *Something greater than gold.*
> —Maurice Carlton

DECORATE THE STAFF

- It is time to decorate the staff. What you use to decorate it will depend on what supplies you gathered.

- **Adult Help:** Your staff can look however you like. Cut pictures from magazines, maps, or decorative paper and attach them with clear packing tape. You can have an adult help you hot glue buttons and fabric on it, too. If you gathered holiday garlands, string, ribbon, or trims, wrap them around the tube and secure with pieces of clear packing tape or duct tape. You can also attach small trinkets to the side of your staff. Have an adult help you do this with hot glue. If the hot glue isn't holding, have an adult help you use the Gorilla Glue. **O P**

- Copy Maurice Carlton's motto (above) on paper and attach with tacky glue or clear packing tape. What do you think he means?

ATTACH THE FINIAL BASE

- Did you decorate your staff using favorite pictures and other cool things? Make sure any glue you used on it is dry. Then it is time to attach the finial base to the staff.

- **Adult Help:** Take the finial and base you made earlier. Have an adult help you cover the center of the base with hot glue. Position the bottom of the base on top of the tube. Hold in place for a few minutes until the glue sets. **Q** **R**

Your burning spear story staff is complete. Take a look at the items you used. Do you know why you chose them? Will you be able to tell others? Take your staff out walking and see if it starts any conversations. Be ready to tell a story about your staff and what its decorations represent. Have fun!

COBWEB VALENTINE

Skill Level 2

A mysterious envelope was slipped under the front door. It was addressed to "My Turtle Dove." Mary reached down excitedly to pick it up. On the back of the envelope was a fancy wax seal. It kept what was inside secret until the envelope was opened. Mary walked into the study to find the silver letter opener on her father's desk. She used it to carefully break the seal. Inside the envelope was a circular valentine. On it was a message from Mary's sweetheart.

Wouldn't it have been faster for him to send Mary a text message? That wasn't possible! Mary received the valentine from her sweetheart in the 1850s, long before cell phones were invented. Hand delivering a note or sending mail were the main forms of written communication. Mary examined the valentine more closely. There was a silk tassel attached to its center. She gently pulled up on the tassel. The delicate paper that was cut into a spiral lifted up from a bed of flowers. Mary saw something! It was a gold heart-shaped locket. Words were printed underneath the locket:

> *I have a message, dear, for you. I say it boldly, for it's true.*
> *Please wear this locket with my hair, with hope that what I feel, we share!*

Mary was thrilled! The valentine and locket were her sweetheart's way of saying how much he liked her.

The Minnesota Historical Society collections include more than a thousand examples of valentines. Some date from the early 1800s. Others are newer, from as recent as the 1990s. Some of the valentines were sent or received by well-known Minnesotans, such as Alexander Ramsey, Minnesota's first territorial governor. There are many kinds of valentines in the collection. Some are organized into themes or categories. Some are romantic, cute, inspirational, or comic. There are even mechanical valentines with moving parts.

In this craft you will make your own old-fashioned, mechanical valentine. The craft pattern is for a cobweb valentine, also called a beehive or flower cage. The design dates back to the Victorian period of the mid- to late 1800s.

You can make your valentine for a friend and then give it to them in person. Or you can mail it. Receiving a mailed message is still a fun surprise today.

Giving people special notes and letters for Valentine's Day began long ago. People in England and the United States sent them in the 1700s. They made handwritten cards. They often decorated the cards with lace and paper flowers. They also drew birds and cherubs on the valentines.

By the early 1900s, sending valentines had become very popular. Something called a Valentine Writer was published during this time. It was a pamphlet containing rhymes and verses for people who wanted to send messages but didn't know what to write. They could rewrite the pamphlet's rhymes and verses to create a valentine.

Supplies

- ☐ Cobweb templates (pages 189–190 or at www.mnhs.org/makinghistory), copied or printed on standard paper

- ☐ **Adult Help:** Base and Inner Circle Base templates (pages 191–192 or at www.mnhs.org/makinghistory), copied or printed on card stock (see note page 8)

- ☐ Envelope template (page 193 or at www.mnhspress.org/makinghistory), enlarged to 250 percent and copied or printed on white or colored 11 × 17–inch paper

  ✔ **TIP:** Your home computer probably can't print out large sheets and may have trouble printing on card stock, so we suggest going to your local copy and print store to make the templates.

- ☐ A surprise item that is small and somewhat flat (examples: ring, locket, candy heart, photo, poem, picture, stickers)

- ☐ Variety of ribbons and lace

- ☐ Variety of scrapbook or decorative paper

- ☐ Variety of embellishments (trinkets, ornaments, buttons, beads)

- ☐ Newspaper or magazines

- ☐ Scissors

- ☐ Markers

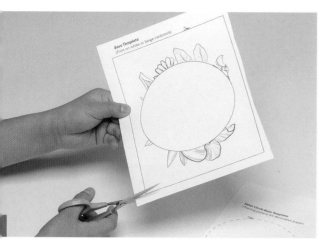

Base template

Cobweb front

- ☐ Needle
- ☐ Thread, a color that matches some of your other supplies, such as the paper and ribbons
- ☐ Scotch tape
- ☐ Tacky white glue
- ☐ Paper plate
- ☐ Toothpicks
- ☐ Glue stick
- ☐ Blue painter's tape or removable glue dots

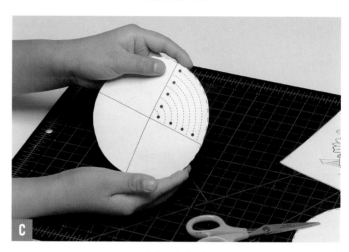

Cobweb back

Optional Supplies

- ☐ Heart paper punch
- ☐ Decorative corner paper punch
- ☐ **Adult Help:** Iron
- ☐ Sticky-backed jewels
- ☐ Doilies
- ☐ Glitter glue

Directions

PREPARE THE PIECES

- Cut out the Base template and the two Cobweb templates. Set aside. A B C
- Use a glue stick to glue the two Cobweb templates together to make a front and back side, with the printed sides showing. Press flat and let dry.

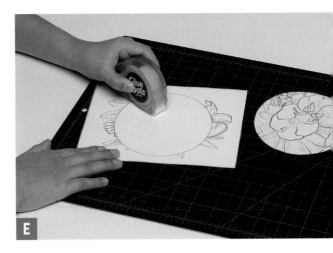

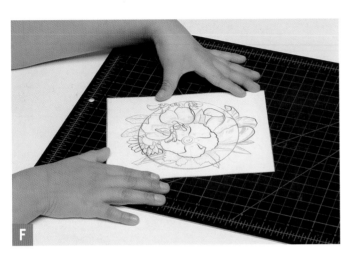

- Place the Cobweb flower side up on top of the Base. Line up the pattern so that the flowers and leaves of the Cobweb match the flowers and leaves on the Base. **D**

- Place four or five *removable* glue dots or small pieces of blue painter's tape on the base. Attach the Cobweb to the Base circle. Make sure everything is in alignment and that the Cobweb circle will not move. **E F**

   ✔ **TIP:** The Cobweb circle will be held down temporarily. This is why removable glue dots and the certain type of tape are *important!* They will be easy to take off later without ripping the paper.

ADD COLOR

- Use markers to color in the flower design on the Cobweb and Base. **G**

- If you gathered glitter glue, squirt some on the paper plate. Use a toothpick to dab and brush the glue lightly where you want some sparkle. Let everything dry for about 15 to 20 minutes.

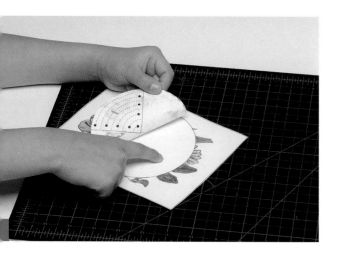

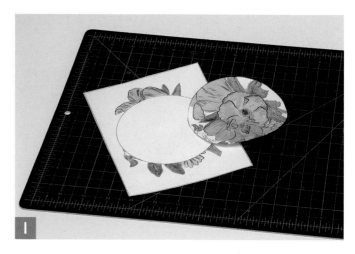

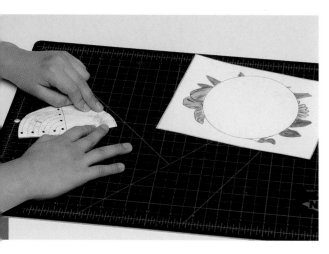

CREATE THE COBWEB

▦ After everything is dry, carefully peel back and lift the colored Cobweb off the Base circle. Completely remove all glue dots or tape. Set the Base aside. **H** **I**

▦ Turn the Cobweb over. Fold and crease the circle in half using the pattern on the back as a guide. The fold should run along one of the solid lines. **J**

▦ Then fold and crease the half circle in half again. Make the fold on one of the solid lines that is beneath the black dots. You should end up with a folded shape that looks like a slice of pizza. The black dots and dotted lines will look like the toppings. **K**

▦ Use a scissors to cut into one side of the folded paper on the dotted lines. *Stop* before you get to the black dot on the opposite side! Do *not* cut all the way across. **L**

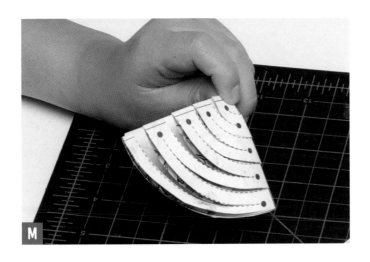

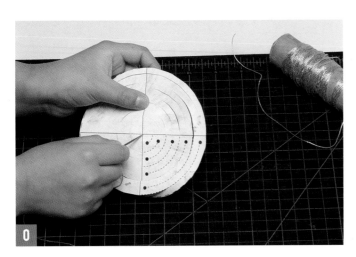

- Now cut the next dotted line starting on the opposite side. *Stop* before you get to the black dot. The cuts on the first and second dotted lines should start on opposite sides.

- Repeat the steps above so that each line starts on the opposite side of the one above it. Make sure you *stop* at the black dots at the end of your cuts each time. **M**

- Unfold the paper very carefully! Gently press and smooth down the circle. It is now a cobweb. **N**

    ✔ **TIP: Adult Help:** To make the Cobweb really smooth and flat, have an adult help you use an iron on it. Set the iron on a low, non-steam setting. Fold a plain sheet of white paper in half. Sandwich the cut Cobweb between the halves, and iron until smooth.

MAKE A PULL STRING

- **Adult Help:** Cut a piece of thread that is about 8 inches long. Have an adult help you thread it through a needle.

- **Adult Help:** Have an adult help you carefully punch a tiny hole in the center of the Cobweb with a needle, on the side with the lines and dots. **O**

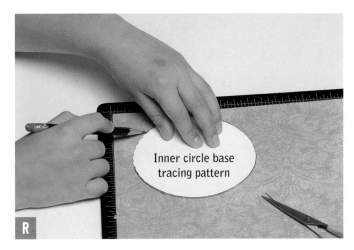

✔ **TIP:** The center of the circle is easy to find. It is where the solid printed lines meet in the middle.

▦ Pull the needle and thread through the center of the circle out through the front.

▦ Knot the thread on the back side of the Cobweb. Then use Scotch tape or a dab of tacky glue to hold the knotted end to the back of the paper. This will keep the thread from pulling all the way through. **P**

▦ Remove the needle from the other end of the thread. Let the thread hang loose.

▦ Find two stickers that are the same design or close to the same size.

▦ Take the loose end of the thread and sandwich the thread between the two stickers so the sticky sides face each other. **Q**

✔ **TIP:** If you gathered sticky-backed jewels, you can also use those for this step.

▦ Use a toothpick to spread a dab of tacky glue around the edges of the stickers or jewels to seal the thread in place.

PLACE THE SURPRISE

▦ Select a piece of scrapbook or decorative paper.

▦ Cut out and trace the Inner Circle Base onto the decorative paper. Cut out the circle. **R**

▦ Take the Base. Place the circle you just cut out in the empty white circle in the middle of the Base. Use a glue stick to glue it down. The design or colored side should be facing up. **S**

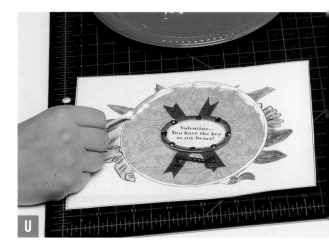

- Now it's time to add a surprise or a message! What would you like to add? It can be a small trinket that you gathered. Or it can be one of the messages shown on page 193. Choose a message and cut it out of the paper.

- If the surprise is a paper message, use the glue stick to glue it onto the decorative paper. Glue it in the center of the circle. If the surprise is a trinket, use Scotch tape or a removable glue dot to attach it to the center. This way, it will stay put but not be ruined by glue when your valentine removes it. **T**

ADD THE COBWEB

- Take the colored, cut Cobweb. Place it on top of the surprise and paper circle.

- Line up the flowers and leaves of the Base with the Cobweb. Remove the Cobweb, but remember exactly where you had it placed. You will be gluing it down in that same spot in the next step.

- Squirt some tacky white glue on the paper plate. Use a toothpick to paint on a line of glue around the base of the decorative paper circle. Make sure it is a thin line! And be sure to stay close to the outer edge of the circle. **U**

- **Adult Help:** Remember exactly how you had the Cobweb placed so the flowers matched up? Have an adult help you place the *outer* ring of the Cobweb onto the glue so that everything lines up. One person should gently pull up the Cobweb's string to stretch the Cobweb's rings out. The other person should press the outer ring down onto the glue.

Valentine's Day falls on February 14. Have you ever sent a valentine to someone? Maybe it was sent by text or e-mail. Or maybe you mailed a greeting card. Many people exchange these messages of affection. It is estimated that a billion people around the world send valentines of some sort.

Smooth down the outer edges of the Cobweb and hold for a few minutes to let the glue dry.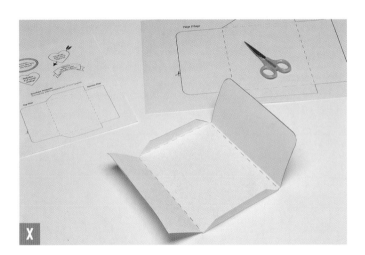

■ Let the Cobweb pull string go. The Cobweb rings should drop and lay somewhat flat on top of the Base. Your surprise in the middle might make some of the rings pop up a little.

■ Your cobweb valentine is almost done. Wait about 15 minutes and let the glue on the outer ring of the Cobweb completely dry.

TEST AND SEND YOUR VALENTINE

■ Time to test your valentine! Pull up gently on the pull string. This should lift the rings of the Cobweb so you can see the hidden surprise inside. The outer ring should stay glued down.

■ Finish decorating the paper borders of the Base. You can use glued-on bits of paper, fabric, lace, doilies, paint, ribbon, jewels, or the hole punches. Have fun! Add the date you made the valentine somewhere on the back. **W**

■ Cut out the enlarged Envelope printout. Fold it as shown on the template. **X**

■ Use a glue stick to glue the sides and edges of the envelope together. Let dry for a few minutes.

■ Insert your cobweb valentine into the envelope and tape it closed.

Some people, such as Mary's sweetheart, give gifts along with a valentine. Long ago, a heart-shaped locket like the one Mary received could even communicate a secret message! If the person giving the locket put a bit of hair inside, this expressed a feeling of "eternal love" to the recipient.

Your cobweb valentine is complete. It is in its envelope and ready to send to your special friend. If you are giving it to them in person, write their name on the front of the envelope. If you are going to mail it, you will also need their address. And a stamp! You may need extra postage to mail your valentine using the U.S. Postal Service. Do you think the person you send it to will be happy and surprised?

DÍA DE LOS MUERTOS NICHO

Skill Level 3

Día de los Muertos means "Day of the Dead" in Spanish. It is the name of a Mexican holiday. It sounds like a spooky, scary day, but it's not! It's a celebration that takes place in the Hispanic community every November 1 and 2. The holiday honors loved ones who have died. The day is filled with traditions that include delicious foods, lively music, and colorful flowers. For Mexican Americans, observing Día de Los Muertos is an important tradition. It helps families stay connected to their culture and ancestors. The holiday is a yearly reunion of family and friends—dead and alive. The celebration rituals and symbols began a long time ago. They can be traced to the time of the Aztec empire, before the Spanish arrived in the Americas in the early 1500s.

Some people might confuse Día de Los Muertos with Halloween, but they are completely different holidays. You won't see witches, black cats, or pumpkins on Día de Los Muertos. But there is one symbol you will see on both holidays: skeletons! Día de Los Muertos skeletons are special. They include recognized characters. One is La Calavera Catrina, a skeleton of a wealthy woman wearing a fancy hat. Her image is everywhere for the holiday: on tablecloths, dishes, and papier-mâché statues. Catrina was made popular by Mexican printmaker Jose Guadalupe Posada in the early 1900s. Her image is meant to remind the living that life is short, so we should enjoy it!

Nichos are another Día de Los Muertos symbolic decoration. They are small shadow boxes with skeleton images on and inside them. The skeletons depict everyday scenes: playing soccer, getting a haircut, playing musical instruments, or getting married. The nichos are found at specialty stores and markets in the United States and Mexico. People often buy them to place on a special altar. This altar is called an *ofrenda,* Spanish for "offering." The ofrenda is set up to honor departed loved ones. Many people display ofrendas on tables in their homes. Sometimes huge ofrendas are set up at a church or community center and everyone adds decorations to them. These decorations include photographs and favorite foods of the departed. Special skulls made of sugar, called *calaveras de azucar,* are also placed on ofrendas. People also place papier-mâché skeletons called *calaveras* on the altars and bread of the dead, which is called *pan de muerto.* Paper cutout designs, or *papel de picado,* and candles are often displayed. So are bright yellow marigold flowers, or *cempasúchil.* These things are what people believe the spirits will enjoy when they return to Earth to visit their living families and friends. People work hard to put together beautiful ofrendas, making and displaying things the dead person enjoyed while alive.

Imagine you are to participate in Día de Los Muertos by making a nicho for an altar. Whom would you like to honor and remember? In this craft, you will make your own nicho! It can be made in honor of someone, or it can be made for your own enjoyment.

Supplies

- ☐ **Adult Help:** Día de los Muertos templates (page 194 or at www.mnhspress.org /makinghistory), copied or printed on card stock (see note page 8)

- ☐ 1 small cardboard box, 4 × 4 × 4 inches (available at craft stores)

- ☐ Heavy cardboard (a cereal box, poster board, or corrugated cardboard)

- ☐ Variety of scrapbooking or decorative paper (sparkle paper works great)

- ☐ Scissors

- ☐ Colored pencils, markers, or crayons

- ☐ Fine-point black marker
- ☐ **Adult Help:** Hot glue gun and hot melt glue
- ☐ Glue stick
- ☐ Tacky white glue
- ☐ Glitter glue
- ☐ Toothpicks
- ☐ Pipe cleaners
- ☐ Tape

Optional Supplies

- ☐ Scrapbooking borders
- ☐ Embroidery appliqués
- ☐ Wrapping paper
- ☐ Variety of fabric trims or ribbon
- ☐ Small flowers (fabric, paper, or artificial)
- ☐ Stickers
- ☐ Glitter
- ☐ Paper plate (if you are going to use glitter)
- ☐ Rhinestones
- ☐ Sequins
- ☐ Old jewelry
- ☐ Small photo (can be of the person to whom you are dedicating the nicho)

    ✔ **TIP:** When reproducing the photo, size it so it fits in the box or paper heart frame pattern included with the templates on page 194.

- ☐ Double-stick tape
- ☐ Foam mounting tape

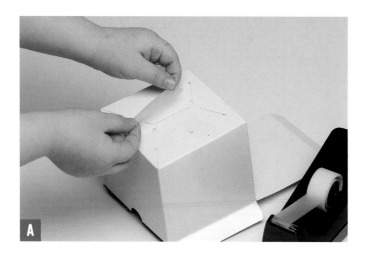

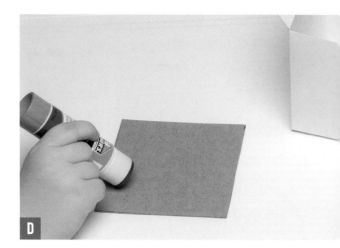

Directions

PREPARE THE BOX

- Assemble the cardboard box. Seal the bottom with tape.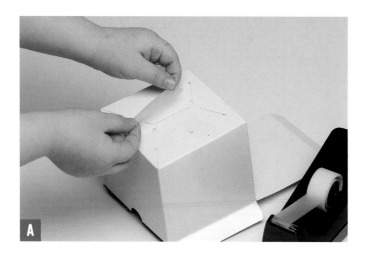

- Trace the bottom of the box onto the cardboard.

- Cut out the cardboard square. Fit the cardboard square inside the bottom of the box. If the square is a bit too big to easily fit, trim its sides as needed.

- Once the cardboard square fits, remove it. Use tacky white glue or the glue stick to glue the square to the inside bottom of the box. **D** **E**

- Lay the box on its side with the lid flat on the table. Use the ruler and a fine-point marker to measure and mark 2 inches into the lid from the center of the box seam line. (See photo F)

- Use the ruler and marker to draw a line from one inside corner of the lid to the mark. Make another line from the opposite inside corner to the mark. The two lines should meet at your mark to make a triangle. **F**

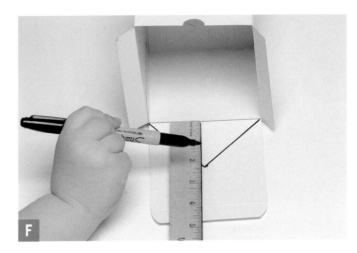

- Carefully cut along the two lines you made. Discard the part of the lid you cut off.

- Set the box on its opposite side. The triangle lid should be at the top, pointing up. The box should be open facing you. Bend the triangle back so it stands up straight. The triangle is the roof of your nicho. **G**

COVER THE SIDE FLAPS IN CARDBOARD

- Measure and mark a rectangle on the heavy cardboard that is 1½ × 4 inches. Cut it out.

- Trace the cardboard rectangle on the cardboard three times. Cut out each rectangle. You should have four pieces of cardboard that are each 1½ × 4 inches. **H**

- Take a piece of the decorative or scrapbook paper you gathered. Trace one of the cardboard rectangles onto the paper four times. Cut out the paper rectangles and set aside.

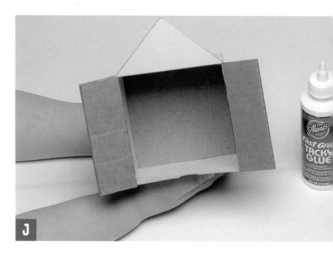

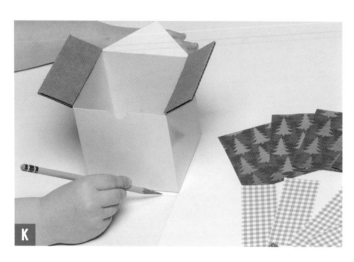

■ Take the four cardboard rectangles. Glue each piece to the front and back of the box's side flaps. It should look like there are two double-sided cardboard doors on the box. **I** **J**

COVER THE BOX IN DECORATIVE PAPER

■ Take the decorative or scrapbook paper you gathered. Trace the bottom of the box onto the papers nine separate times. You can use different patterns and colors of paper if you like.

■ Cut out all nine squares. Set aside. **K**

■ Lay the box on its side on top of a piece of decorative paper so that the triangle flap is lying flat on the paper. Trace the sides of the triangle flap. Remove the box and use the ruler to connect the two lines to make a triangle on the paper. Cut the triangle out. **L**

■ Lay the box on its side again on top of decorative paper so that the triangle flap is lying flat on the paper. Trace the sides of the triangle flap again. Remove the box. This time, use the ruler to extend the two diagonal lines to make them each ¼ inch longer. Then use the ruler to connect the two lines and make a triangle. Cut the triangle out. **M**

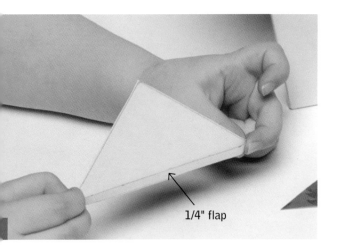

1/4" flap

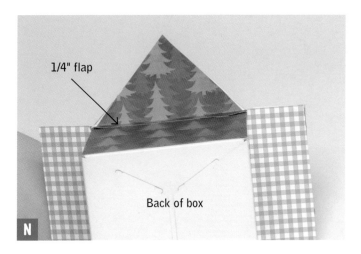

1/4" flap

Back of box

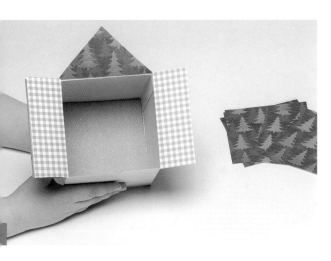

- You will now have one triangle that is the same size as the box's triangle flap and one that is a bit bigger. Take the bigger paper triangle and use the glue stick to glue it to the *back* side of the triangle flap on the box. Line up the diagonal sides. Where the bottom part overlaps, push it into the seam where the triangle flap and the top of the box meet. Glue the extra bit of paper to the top of the box. This step will help keep the triangle flap standing nice and straight. N

- Glue the other triangle to the *front* of the triangle flap on the box. O

- Glue all the paper pieces you cut out onto the inside and outside of the box. You don't need to cover the bottom of the box that you taped together at the beginning of the craft.

- Decorate the box. You can use the glue stick or white tacky glue to add decorative trims or ribbon, beads, or stickers. Add any decorative border or appliqués you gathered. Use a toothpick to dab and brush glittery glue on the box wherever you like. You can also use craft glue or tape to attach any pieces of wrapping paper or other decorations.

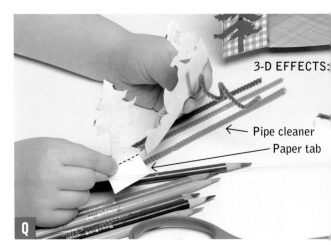

3-D EFFECTS:

← Pipe cleaner
← Paper tab

PREPARE THE SKELETONS OR HEARTS

- Take the Día de los Muertos templates. Enlarge as needed. Cut out the images that you like.

- Use colored pencils, markers, or crayons to color the black-and-white images. Use the glitter glue or sparkly paper to add highlights. **P**

CREATE 3-D EFFECTS

You're almost ready to place the images in the box. But first, you can make some of them 3-D by cutting a paper tab or bending a pipe cleaner.

- Choose an image you want to appear inside the box. **Q**

- Paper tabs: Cut a piece of card stock that is as wide as the bottom of one of your images. Glue or tape the very bottom of the image to the top surface of the card stock. Bend the image at the bottom to make it stand up.

- Pipe cleaners: Bend a pipe cleaner into an accordion-like fold. Attach one end of the pipe cleaner to the back of the image with tape.

- **Adult Help:** Put the image (which is attached to the tab or pipe cleaner) inside the box to see how far you want it to stand out from the back of the box. If you used a pipe cleaner, trim it to the length that you like. If you made a tab, be sure the base is trimmed and fits inside the box. Use a dollop of hot glue to attach the pipe cleaner or tab to the inside of the box. Your image should stand up and stick out toward you.

- Use pipe cleaners or tabs and hot glue to make other images look 3-D. You can stick some popping off the flaps, too. Or glue the image right to the flaps. **R**

▓ Continue to add decorations and details to the box until you feel it's finished. Write the date somewhere on the back or the bottom of the box.

Your Día de los Muertos nicho is complete. Take a minute to look it over. What is your favorite part? Whom did you make it for? What do you think their favorite part would be? You can display your nicho at home. You might even want to gather more items and set up an ofrenda!

"RIDE THE WAVES" BOAT AND SKIER

Skill Level 3

Have you ever read the children's book *If You Give a Mouse a Cookie* by Laura Numeroff? If you have, you know how one thing leads to another. In the book, the mouse first wants a cookie. Then he wants some milk. Then he wants a straw, and then a napkin. This goes on and on until the end of the book, when the mouse wants a cookie again!

What if you were to write a book like that about how Minnesota lakes formed? If you wrote it in the same style as the mouse and cookie book, it might sound like this:

If you have thousands of years of cold weather, then you are going to have a lot of ice. If you have a lot of ice, that ice is going to get heavy. If the ice gets really heavy, the weight of it will melt the bottom layer. If the bottom layer melts, the ice will move. If it moves, it's going to pick up a lot of rocks. If the ice picks up rocks, it will scrape the earth and make deep potholes. When the weather gets warmer, the ice will melt. When the ice melts, the potholes will fill with water. When the filled-up potholes are really big, a lake is created. When 10,000 lakes have formed, that area is called Minnesota!

The glaciers described above are geologic forces. They shaped Minnesota's landscape over the last 75,000 years. Glaciers are huge masses of ice. One especially big, ancient glacier was known as the Laurentide Ice Sheet. Climate changes caused the ice sheet to grow larger and larger as more ice froze on it. Soon it covered all of Canada! It also covered the northeastern United States and much of the Upper Midwest, including Minnesota. This glacier moved very, very slowly as it grew. It pushed around a lot of rock and soil as it moved, scarring the land. When the Laurentide Ice Sheet melted, many of the holes it carved filled up with the water. These became rivers and lakes.

Minnesota had a lot of holes that became lakes—11,842 of them! And if you have a lot of lakes, that means a lot of chances to have fun in water.

Motor boats were invented in Germany in 1886, but an American made them faster. John Hacker designed a boat with a V-shaped bottom, or "hull." V-shaped hulls are faster because they skim on top of the water instead of pushing through the water.

In 1922, all those fast boats gave an 18-year-old Minnesotan an idea. His name was Ralph Samuelson, and he lived near Lake Pepin. He thought it would be fun to ski on water, tied behind a fast boat. Ralph tried with a pair of snow skis, but they didn't work. Next, Ralph made a pair of skis from 8-foot pine boards. Would that work better than the narrow skis? What if he bent the front of the pine skis up? He took his mother's cooking pot to boil some water, and he stuck the tips in to make them soft enough to bend. Ralph and his brother tried out the new skis for a couple days. On July 2, 1922, they got it right. They found that if Ralph leaned back so the tips pointed up out of the water, the fast boat would pull him up. There he was, skiing on top of the water! Water skiing was born that day, right here in Minnesota.

Ralph Samuelson with his original water skis, 1966

Next time you're out on a glacier-created Minnesota lake, in a fast boat designed by an American, think about a young Minnesotan named Ralph Samuelson. He invented one more way to have fun in water.

Here's your chance to celebrate Minnesota's lake culture. You can make a water-skier who cuts through the water behind a "battery-powered" boat. It's really a weight-powered boat, and the battery doesn't even have to work! The battery is a rolling weight to make the boat glide. A water ramp (complete with spray) provides stability. That way, your skillful skier won't tip over.

This is a fun project to do with an adult. You can choose to make all three parts, just the skier, or just the boat. It's up to you. Read on to find out how.

Supplies

☐ **Adult Help:** Body, Head, Skis, Ski Straps, Ramp, Ramp Extension, Boat Exterior, Boat Back Extension, Benches, and Battery Box templates (pages 195–202 or at www.mnhspress.org/makinghistory), copied or printed on heavy, 100-pound card stock (see note page 8)

✔ **TIP:** Three of the templates are two sided. (1) Print the Water Skier Reverse Side on one side of a piece of card stock, and print the Water Skier Heads and Water Skier Body on the other. (2) Print the Boat Exterior on one side of a piece of card stock, and print the Boat on the other side. (3) Print the Boat Exterior on one side of a piece of card stock, and print the Boat Extension with Skis and Ski Straps on the other side.

☐ 2 scissors: 1 small with sharp tips and 1 with longer blades

☐ Glue stick or craft glue (3M Quick-Dry Adhesive works well for this craft)

☐ Spring-loaded clothespins

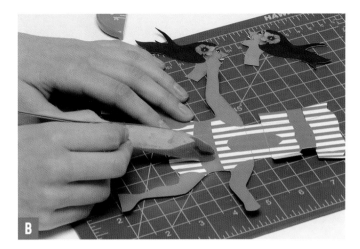

- ☐ C battery (a dead/used battery is okay)

- ☐ Ruler

- ☐ Paper drinking straw (available at craft stores)

- ☐ Butter knife or bone folder

- ☐ **Adult Help:** Hobby or craft knife and a cutting mat

- ☐ Piece of corrugated cardboard (about 4 × 6 inches)

- ☐ String

- ☐ Pencil

Optional Supplies

- ☐ An old magazine for gluing

- ☐ Toothpicks

- ☐ French curve

- ☐ A board or piece of cardboard (3 feet or more) to use as a ramp

Directions

MAKE THE WATER-SKIER

- ▦ Roughly cut out the Body template, and then carefully trim on the outlines. Cut out the two Head templates on the outlines. Set the heads aside.

- ▦ Take the Body cutout. You will score all four of the curved, dotted lines by pressing down with your scoring tool hard enough to indent the paper but not so hard that you cut into it. This step will make it easier to fold the paper along the line. **B**

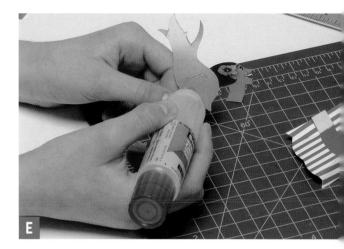

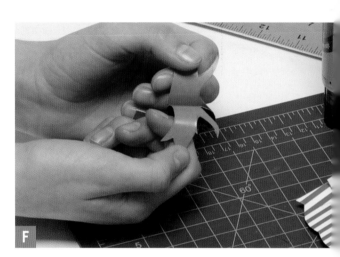

✔ **TIP:** Scoring curved lines is harder than straight ones, so draw a curved line on a scrap of card stock first to practice.

✔ **TIP:** If you have a French curve, which is a special drawing tool, you can match the curve of the ruler with the curve of the score line. Then you can run your scoring tool alongside it.

▥ After the lines are scored, fold them. To fold a curved line, place the fingertips of one hand directly under the score line. Press down with the fingers of your other hand to fold along the line. Start in the middle and work your way out. After you bend along the lines, you can crease it a little more by gently pinching the edge. **C** (page 131)

▥ Note the solid lines on the front sides of the Body that run horizontally along the swimsuit lines. Cut along those four lines. Do *not* cut into your dotted fold lines. The cuts will divide each front side section into three little flaps.

▥ Score the two fold lines across the shoulders. Fold them. Now you have a rectangle with a slit mark in the middle. That will become the base for the neck. **D**

▥ Glue the two unprinted sides of the Heads together in the head and neck area only. Leave the hair free. Make sure the Head outlines match up. **E**

▥ Fan out and curl the ends of the hair so it looks like it's blowing in the wind. Gently curve the hair over your finger or a pencil. Set the glued-together Head aside. **F**

▥ **Adult Help:** Lay the Body printed side up on a cutting mat. Ask for adult help to cut the vertical neck slit with a craft knife. Start with one slice along the line. Make sure the cut doesn't go past the ends! Insert the Head into the neck slit. Adjust the length or width of the slit until the neck goes smoothly into it. Remove the Head and set aside. **G**

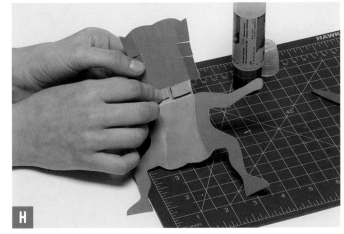

■ Flip the skier over. Cut and glue two small pieces of cardboard to go on either side of the neck slit. They should fit between the shoulder folds and be close to the slit line so the Head won't flop from side to side when it's inserted later. **H**

■ *Read these directions to do a construction "rehearsal" before you glue:*

- Hold the skier in front of you with the back half of the skier in your left hand. The neck section and the front section will be on the right. Notice the curved fold lines on the back.

- Bend the front down and back. Tuck the front half into the inside back section. The arms and legs will bend forward at the curved line. Now bring the legs and arms forward to hug the front body. The cuts you made along the bathing suit let the front flex a little so that it fits into the curve of the back body.

- You can see that the bathing suit matches up. Notice that the bottom edge of the back leg lines up with the bottom of the bathing suit. It comes together in an inverted-V shape.

- You will end up with a boxlike shape that will be the skier's body. The neck slit will be at the top. Is that clear to you? If it is, grab your glue and a clothespin and get ready to glue!

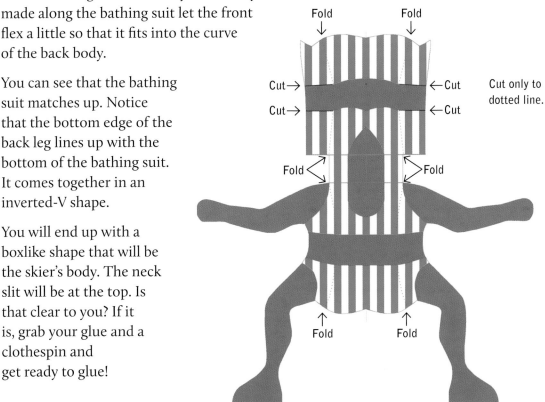

 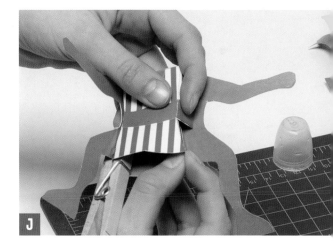

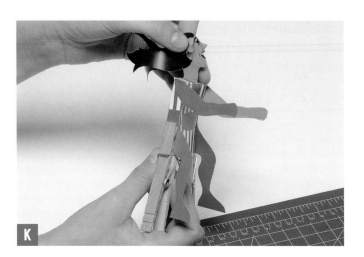 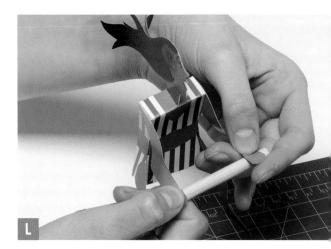

- Start with the front body. Lay it printed side up on your work surface. Glue the three flaps with glue or glue stick. Tuck the front section into the back. Line up the inverted-V shape on one side and clamp with a clothespin. **I**

- Push back gently on the "skin section" of the front to press it into the back curve. Put a finger inside against the top of the glued part. Gently press against the shoulder until you're sure the glue sticks.

- When that side is stuck, repeat with the flaps on the other side. **J**

- Insert the neck into the neck slit. Push down until the slit lines up with the horizontal line on the neck. If the slit is too loose, pull the Head out and use a toothpick to insert a little glue along the edge of the slit before reinserting the neck. **K**

- Take the paper straw. Measure and cut a piece that is 2½ inches long. This will be the horizontal tow rope handle.

- Gently rotate the skier's hands down to hold the handle. Glue the hands to the outside edges of the straw. It should look like the water-skier is holding a tow rope. **L**

- Your water-skier is complete. Set her aside as you build the other items.

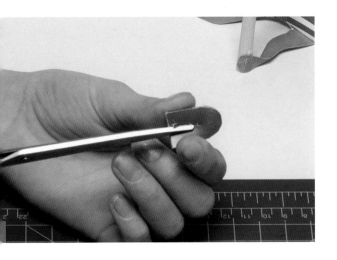

MAKE THE WATER SKIS

- Cut out the Skis and Ski Straps templates.

- Take a piece of corrugated cardboard. Do you see which way the ribs are running? Position the Skis and Ski Straps on the cardboard so the ribs of the cardboard run across the Skis, not down. Glue the Skis and Ski Straps to the cardboard. Cut out these four pieces.

- Take the Ski Straps. Cut into the marked line with a scissors. Set aside.

- **Adult Help:** Take the Skis. There are matching red straps. Ask an adult to use a craft knife to cut slits there. The feet of the water-skier will slide into these slits. Check to make sure that the feet will fit. If the slits need to be longer, cut them a bit more.

- Lay a pencil across the front tip of one of the Skis. As you press down, roll the cardboard back over it to curve the end up. Repeat with the other Ski.

- Insert the feet of the water-skier into the Ski slots.

- Take the Ski Straps. Glue the unprinted side. Slide the cut slits around the skier's feet and press down firmly.

- Your skier is ready to ski. Now she needs some water!

MAKE THE WATER RAMP

- Roughly cut out the Ramp and Ramp Extension, and then trim along the outlined edges. Don't worry if you don't cut the wavy edges perfectly. But make sure you cut the straight areas exactly on the line. They have to fold and fit together in later steps.

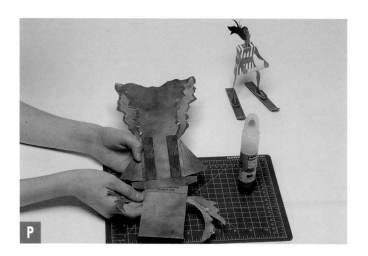

▦ Add glue to the Ramp Extension tab where it is marked. Place the Ramp on top. Line up the lines, and press down to secure. **P**

▦ When the glue is dry, score and fold along all the fold lines, including the ones next to the water sprays. **Q**

▦ *Read these directions and look at photo R before you glue anything else:*

- Do a folding "run-through" without glue so that you can see how the front of the Ramp folds back under itself.

- There are two triangles on either side of the skis. The triangles will get folded in. The outside triangles will end up along the bottom. The middle triangles will form an incline, like a ski jump.

- There is a rectangle with tabs between the skis and the water sprays. These tabs fold down and get tucked into the inside of the folded triangles and glued. The triangles will fold in over the tabs.

- The rectangle ends up being the front of the incline as you fold the section with the sprays underneath. It will be taped to the bottom. The sprays stick out the sides, printed side down.

- The two sprays get folded up and glued to the outside of the incline.

- Clear? Okay, let's get to work!

FOLDING DIAGRAM

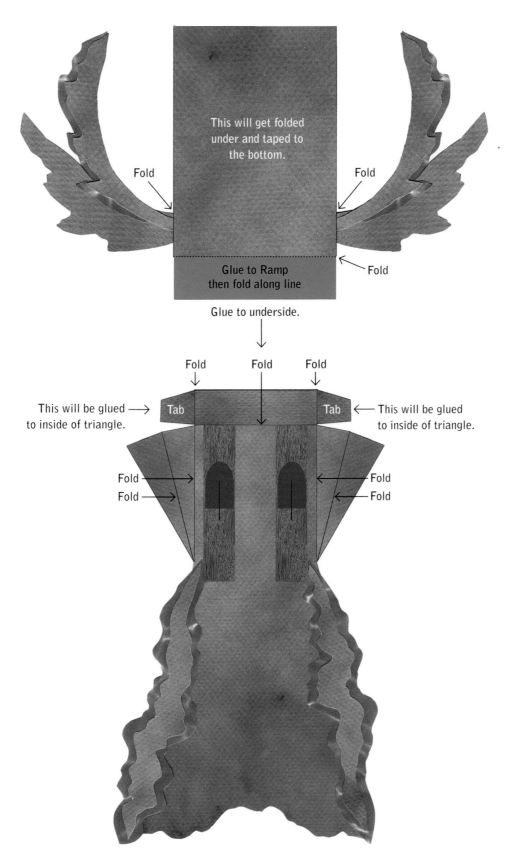

This will get folded
under and taped to
the bottom.

Fold

Fold

Fold

**Glue to Ramp
then fold along line**

Glue to underside.

Fold

Fold

Fold

This will be glued
to inside of triangle.

Tab

Tab

This will be glued
to inside of triangle.

Fold

Fold

Fold

Fold

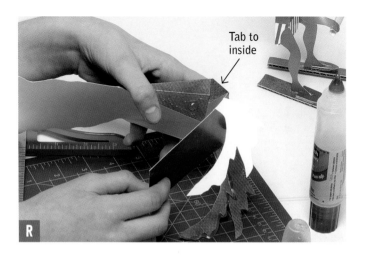

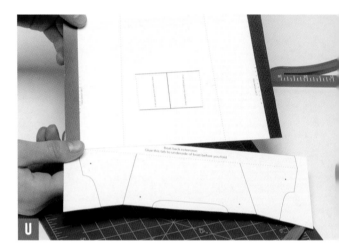

- Glue the printed side of the tabs. Fold them down, and as you do that, fold the triangles down over them. Press the glued tabs to make certain they're stuck to the inside of the triangles. **R**

- Fold the extension (with the sprays) to the underside.

- Tape the back edge of the extension to the bottom of the Ramp. **S**

- Fold the water sprays up and glue them to the sides of the Ramp.

- Glue the water-skier and skis onto the Ramp as marked. The skis will extend beyond the Ramp. **T**

- Set these aside as you make the boat.

MAKE THE BOAT

- Cut out Boat, Benches, and Battery Box templates.

- Cut the Boat Back Extension along the long straight horizontal edge.

- Glue the Boat Back Extension to the bottom of the Boat back. Make sure you position it exactly on the line. **U**

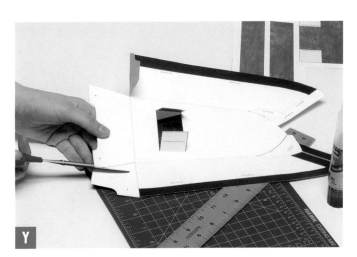

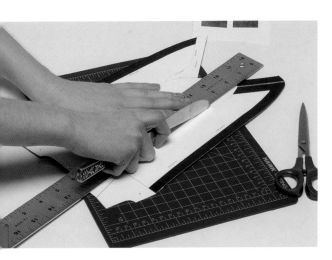

- When the glue is dry, score a line along the horizontal seam you just glued. Press down with your scoring tool along that line, right at the joined area between the two pieces.

- Trim around the rest of the Boat Back Extension.

- Cut into the curved area of the bow (the front of the boat) along the solid lines. Do not cut the dotted lines. **V**

- **Adult Help:** Ask an adult to cut the solid lines of the Battery Box opening. Score the dotted lines. Open the little doors. These flaps will later be glued to the inside of the Battery Box. **W**

- Place the edge of a ruler along one of the dotted fold lines that run from the front to the back of the Boat. Score it. Repeat with the second diagonal line. **X**

- Cut the solid diagonal lines of the Boat Back Extension. Don't cut into the horizontal seam! Fold these three pieces forward and run your fingers across the top to crease firmly. Fold the diagonal scored lines to form the sides of the boat. **Y**

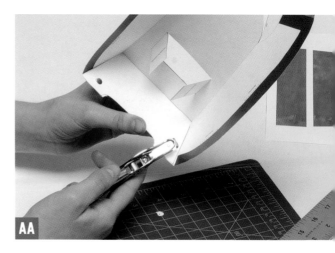

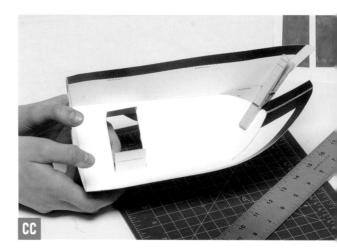

- Put glue on the two unprinted side sections of the extension. Fold them to the outside of the middle section. This will form the back side of the boat. The two sides will meet in the middle. Clamp them with clothespins until the glue dries. **Z**

- When the glue dries, punch holes at the marked dots at the back of the Boat. You will attach the tow rope there later. **AA**

- Next, glue the bow, or front, of the Boat together. Coat the rounded triangular shape on the right with glue. Then place it under the bow along the dotted lines. Clamp with a clothespin until dry. **BB** **CC**

- Glue the areas on the left side of the bow where marked. Ease it into position under the right side of the bow. Line up the line and the top edges. Clamp with a clothespin until the glue is dry. Set boat aside. **DD**

- Take the Battery Box printout. Score and fold the dotted lines. Cut the solid lines. **EE** **FF**

- Fold and glue the lighter colored tabs to the inside of the box. Let the glue dry. **GG**

- On the Boat, glue the flaps of the battery box opening. Place the Battery Box over them and press the flaps to the inside of the box. **HH** **II**

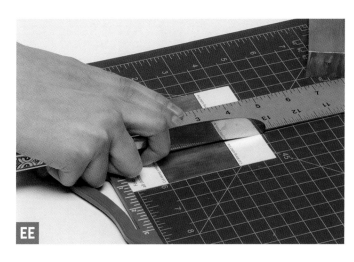

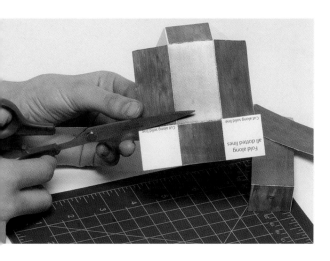

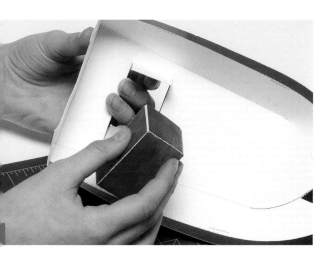

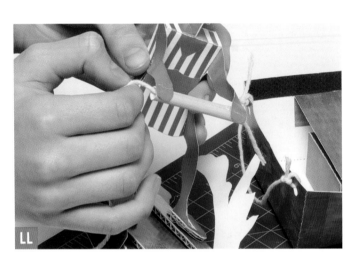

- Take the Benches. Fold them along the dotted lines. One bench at a time, match the letters on the benches to the letters found on the inside of the Boat, underneath the colored rail. Glue the folded tabs to the sides. **JJ**

- Measure and cut a piece of string that is 7 inches long. Tie one end of the string to one hole that you punched in the back. Tie the other end to the other hole. When you pull the string at the center, it will form a triangle. **KK**

- Measure and cut another piece of string that is 11 inches long.

- Take the water-skier. Thread one end of the string through the straw in her hands. When it comes out the other end of the straw, tie the string together in front of the handle. **LL**

- Tie the other end of the string to the back of the boat string to attach the water-skier to the boat. **MM**

Your water-skier, ramp, and boat are complete. Now, if you found a board or piece of cardboard for your ramp, set something under one end to raise it. Place the boat, ramp, and skier at the high end of the board or cardboard. Take the C battery. Place it in the battery box underneath the boat. Now let it go. The boat will move down the ramp, pulling along the water-skier and waves!

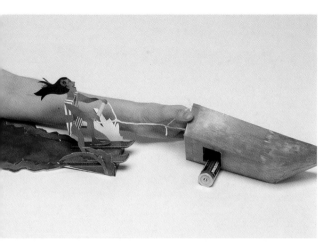

PAUL BUNYAN ACTION TOY

Skill Level 4

I t had been quiet and cold for so many months that year, the Winter of the Blue Snow. It was so cold the words froze in midair! No words, no sounds, no howling winds. Not even a "Please pass the peas" was heard. But now the ice was breaking up. All the sounds, all the words suddenly came alive! Snores, grunts, the bark of a dog, a "howdy do" came crashing down around the loggers. The sounds piled up at their feet and made a terrible racket. "Coldest winter ever," the oldest lumberjacks muttered. "Never seen anythin' like it."

The extreme cold was not the only unusual thing about that winter. Nor was the blue snow. Something blue changed one lumberjack's life that season. That was the year Paul Bunyan, a lumberjack of legendary size and strength, found Babe. He was out in the brutal cold one day when he stumbled upon something. There in the snowdrifts, Paul found a baby ox. That little ox was jumping up and snorting, mad as could be, trying to see over the big blue snowdrifts. It is

Paul Bunyan and Babe, postcard, 1940

a surprise Paul saw him at all—this ox was as blue as the snow! Paul saved him from the cold. He took him home and warmed him up. He named him Babe the Blue Ox.

Throughout the silent winter, Paul took care of Babe. Under his care, Babe grew—oh boy, he grew! Soon he was big enough and strong enough to help Paul. Together they cleared acre after acre of forest. Together they pulled out the twists and turns of the logging roads, making them straight. Paul and Babe the Blue Ox. Best friends forever.

The story of Paul and Babe is a tall tale. A tall tale is a story with bigger-than-life details. It's like looking at your shadow on a late summer day: A small boy becomes a giant. A gentle wave of his hand sweeps across the yard. Some of these Paul Bunyan stories became more unbelievable with every telling. Where did these stories come from? Were they made up? Or were they exaggerated tales of especially strong and powerful lumberjacks? Some people think the stories began in logging camps in Canada. Others think they came from Wisconsin. Many people believe the stories—and Paul and Babe themselves—were from Minnesota.

People pose with Paul Bunyan and Babe at Bemidji's 1937 winter carnival

Minneapolis illustrator William Laughead helped make Paul and Babe stories popular. He helped them move out of the thick pine forests and logging camps of Minnesota. He gave the character of Paul a face in 1914 when he drew him as the logo for the Red River Lumber Company when it moved to California. Brochures were created featuring fantastic stories of Paul and Babe. The brochures were published and republished, until soon they swept the country.

In the 1930s, the lumber industry slowed down. But stories about the lumberjack Paul and his sidekick Babe were still very popular. At the same time, tourism was growing. People were beginning to travel the United States. Many knew the stories of Paul and Babe. State tourist industries created roadside attractions of the pair across the country, from Maine to Oregon. Many of these huge statues of Paul and Babe still stand today—several in Minnesota!

In this craft, you'll make your very own Paul statue. But it will be unique. Unlike the huge statues, this one will fit in your hand—a small version of a giant legend! Your version will also be special in another way. It will be a *moving* creation. Read on to find out how to make a Paul Bunyan figure that actually chops wood!

Today there are sightings of Paul Bunyan and Babe the Blue Ox on the shores of Lake Bemidji in Minnesota. Giant statues of the pair have been standing there since 1937. The statue of Paul was modeled after Bemidji's mayor at the time, Earl Bucklen. But the statue was much larger than Earl! The statue of Paul is 18 feet tall and weighs 2.5 tons. It took 737 hours to build. It is made from wood, wire, concrete, and plaster. Next to the giant logger is a huge statue of Babe. It weighs even more than Paul: 5 tons!

Supplies

- ☐ **Adult Help:** *For both versions:* Paul Bunyan Base, Body Spacer, and Arm Washer templates (page 205 or at www.mnhspress.org/makinghistory), copied or printed on card stock (see note page 8)

- ☐ **Adult Help:** *For Cardboard Paul Bunyan:* Right Body, Left Body, Right Arm, Left Arm, Right Leg, Left Leg, and Ax templates (page 203 or at www.mnhspress.org/makinghistory), copied or printed on card stock (see note page 8)

- ☐ **Adult Help:** *For Illustrated Paul:* Right Body, Left Body, Right Arm, Left Arm, Right Leg, Left Leg, and Ax illustrated cutouts (page 204 or at www.mnhspress.org/makinghistory), copied or printed on card stock (see note page 8)

- ☐ Scissors

- ☐ Cardboard (see note page 148)

  - ☐ Thick corrugated cardboard

  - ☐ Thinner corrugated cardboard

  - ☐ Poster board or a large, flattened gift box

- ☐ **Adult Help:** Hot glue gun and hot melt glue

- ☐ Ruler

- ☐ Pencil

- ☐ **Adult Help:** Sharp, pointed tool to make small holes, like the point of a drawing compass or a small nail

- ☐ ¼–inch hole punch

- ☐ Something with a hole in the middle to use for the weight pendulum: a wooden toy wheel or 2 washers, about the weight of 3 nickels

- ☐ Needle-nose pliers

- ☐ 10-inch piece of 18-gauge wire

- ☐ Bead with hole large enough for wire to go through

- ☐ Linen, upholstery, or button thread

- ☐ Sewing needle

- ☐ Glue stick or craft glue

- ☐ ⅝– or ¾–inch flat button, about ⅛ inch thick

- ☐ Spring-loaded clothespin or other clamp

- ☐ Cutting mat or cutting board

Optional Supplies

- ☐ ⅛–inch hole punch

- ☐ **Adult Help:** Hobby or craft knife

- ☐ T-square ruler

- ☐ Markers, crayons, colored pencils

NOTE ON CARDBOARD

Because this is a recycled craft, you'll use a lot of common things around your house. You'll need three different kinds of cardboard. The first, which will be used for Paul's face and body, is lighter-weight cardboard, like a cereal or gift box or poster board. Everything else will be cut from corrugated cardboard. We used a thinner corrugated cardboard for the arms and legs. We chose a thicker corrugated cardboard for the base, log, body spacers, and shoulder washer. Look at the picture to see examples. You may have to try a couple kinds to find one that you can cut without too much trouble.

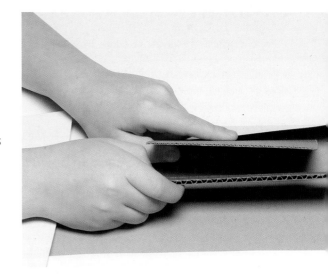

Look at your templates or illustrated cutouts to see how much cardboard you need. You will also have to cut a long piece of the thicker corrugated cardboard to roll up into the log. It needs to be at least 2 × 20 inches, with the ribs (see page 7) of the cardboard running across the rectangle, not along the long side. That will make it easier to roll up.

NOTE ON OPTIONS

There are two versions you can make for Paul. We provide *cutouts* to cut and glue onto cardboard for an illustrated version. In that one, all Paul's features and clothes are already printed on the pieces. We provide templates, or patterns, to trace onto cardboard for the other one. That way, you get to decide what Paul looks like. Use paints, markers—even add your own profile photo! Both versions use the same templates and measurements for everything else that is made. Except for a picture at the beginning of the directions, we will only show the version that you decorate yourself.

Directions

PREPARE THE TEMPLATES AND CUTOUTS

- ▮ Cut out all templates and illustrated pieces for your version. Use a pencil to lightly mark the names of each on the back so that you don't mix them up. **A**

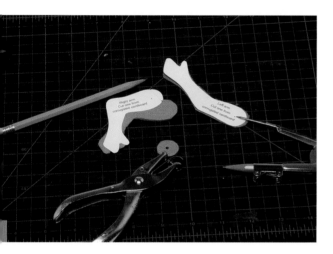

PREPARE THE BODIES, ARMS, LEGS, AND AX

Plain cardboard Paul Bunyan

▦ Trace the Left and Right Body templates onto poster board or cereal box cardboard. Cut them out. Mark "right" and "left" on the back. **B**

▦ Transfer the position marks. There are small dots at the shoulders. Lay the Body templates back on top of each piece. Line them up. Take something with a sharp point. Transfer the position markings onto the cardboard by poking a hole through the dot. There is also a row of position marks at the bottom of the Left Body. Mark them in the same way. Set aside. **C**

▦ Trace the Arms, Legs, and Ax templates onto the lighter-weight corrugated cardboard. Cut them out. Mark their names on the back side.

▦ Lay the Arm templates back on top of the cardboard arms. Mark the dots and use an ⅛–inch punch or your sharp tool to make holes through the arms. At the top of the right arm, mark the "needle insertion" line.

▦ Add any details you want to body, face, arms, and legs.

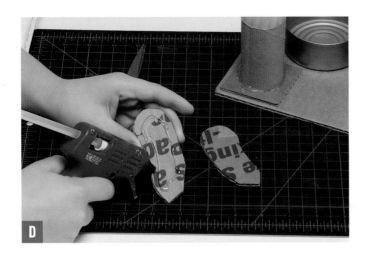

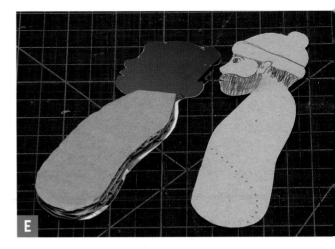

Illustrated Paul Bunyan

▩ Use a glue stick to glue the Left and Right Body cutouts onto poster board or lightweight cardboard. Cut them out. Mark their names on the back.

▩ Use a glue stick to glue the Arms, Legs, and Ax cutouts onto lighter-weight corrugated cardboard. Cut them out.

> ✔ **TIP:** You can color the back sides of the legs and arms with black marker so that they aren't "cardboard color."

▩ Take the two arms. Use an ⅛–inch punch or other sharp tool to poke a hole at the dot on the shoulders. Mark their names on the back. Set aside.

Both Versions

▩ Trace the Arm Washer template and the two Body Spacer templates onto the thicker corrugated cardboard. Cut out. Make a hole in the arm washer at the dot. Set aside.

▩ **Adult Help:** Take the two body spacers. Use a glue gun to glue a line on one body spacer. Immediately place the other one on top of the glue, lining up the edges and pressing down. **D**

▩ Next, sandwich the glued spacer between the left and right body:

- **Adult Help:** Lay one body onto your work surface with the wrong side facing up (poster board side of the illustrated one, or undecorated side of the plain one). The spacer is slightly smaller than the body. Line up the spacer along the bottom edge of the body. Place hot glue on the spacer, and press it in place on the body. **E**

- **Adult Help:** Next you'll glue the other body onto the spacer to sandwich it. First, line up the two bodies to match. Then use a glue gun to add a line of glue along the top of the spacer. Immediately press the body onto it. **F**

- **Adult Help:** Put a dot of hot glue between the two heads to stick them together. One little dot is all you need. **G**

▩ Lay a scrap piece of thick corrugated cardboard on your cutting mat or board. Lay the

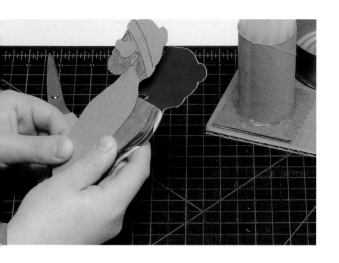

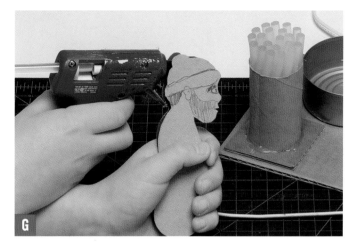

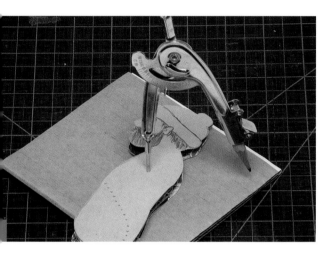

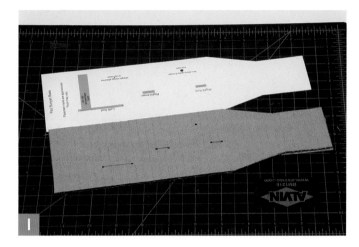

body on top. Use your sharp point to poke a hole through all the layers where you marked the dot at the shoulder. Make sure your tool is straight up and down. Set aside when you are done. **H**

The rest of the directions are identical for both versions.

CUT THE BASE, LOG, SUPPORT STRIPS, AND ATTACHMENT SQUARE

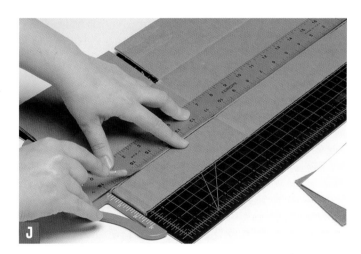

- Trace the Base template onto a piece of thick corrugated cardboard. Cut it out. Transfer the placement markings onto the cardboard in the same way you marked the arms and body. You do not have to mark log placement. **I**

- **Adult Help:** Measure and mark a long rectangle 2 inches wide and 20 inches long. The ribs of the cardboard should run across the 2 inches, not down the long way. Cut this piece out with scissors, or ask an adult to cut it with a craft knife on a cutting mat. **J**

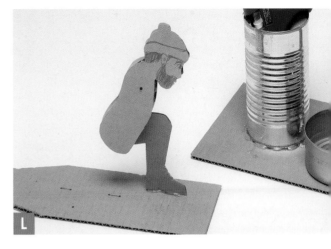

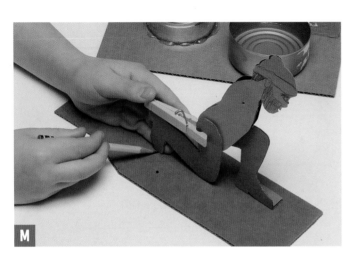

■ Also cut three support strips from the corrugated cardboard. Measure and cut two that are ½ × 3 inches and one that is ½ × 2 inches. Set aside.

■ Cut one ½ × ½–inch square. Set aside.

ATTACH THE LEGS AND BODY TO THE BASE

■ **Adult Help:** Take the left leg and the body. The curve of the top of the leg should line up with the placement holes poked into the cardboard. Hot glue the leg to the body. K

■ **Adult Help:** Now you'll hot glue the foot to the base at the left foot placement line. Glue along the placement line and immediately press the bottom of the foot into it. If it seems wobbly after the glue cools, you can glue the 2-inch support to the left of the foot. L

■ Place the right leg along the right side of the body as you position it onto the base. Make sure the leg touches the base at both the toe and the knee. The position marks on the base may be slightly different. Slide the leg back and forth until it looks like Paul Bunyan is kneeling. Use a clothespin to hold the leg in place.

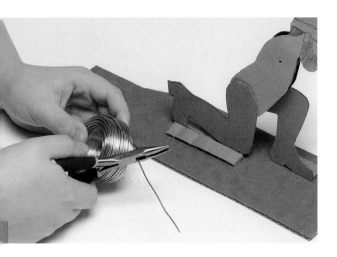

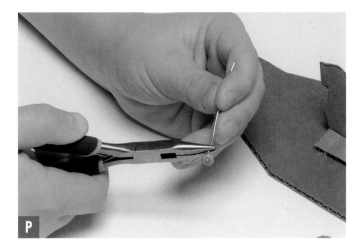

- Use a pencil to mark the spots where the right foot and knee touch the base. Draw a line along the rounded top of the leg to mark where it touches the body. Remove the clothespin. **M**

- **Adult Help:** Lift the right leg up slightly. Hot glue the bottom edge of the foot and the knee to the base at your pencil marks. Glue the 3-inch rectangle against the right side of the foot to hold securely.

- **Adult Help:** Slightly pull the top of the leg away from the body. Hot glue the leg to the body. **N**

ATTACH THE ARMS AND CHECK THE SWING

- ✔ **TIP:** This is the trickiest part of the project. You may have to adjust the wire on the right side a little, so adult help is a really good idea.

- Cut a 4-inch length of the 18-gauge wire using the needle-nose pliers. There is a built-in wire cutter where the blades meet. **O**

- Thread one end of the wire through the bead. Use the pliers to twist the end of the wire around the bead to secure. **P**

- Now place the base/body in front of you. Paul should face forward, away from you. (See Q, page 154.) You are going to attach the arms to both sides of the body. Before you start, place the left arm and the arm washer on the left side. Place the button and the right arm on the right side.

- Poke the wire through the hole in the left arm. Pull through until the bead hits the arm.

- Take the shoulder washer and thread it on the wire.

- Push the wire through the hole in the left side of the body so that it comes out on the right side of the body.

- Thread the button onto the wire so it is touching the right side of the body.

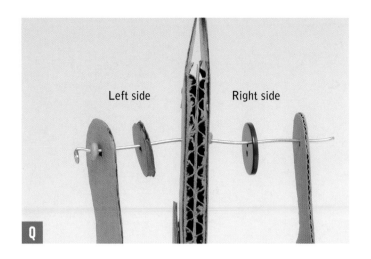

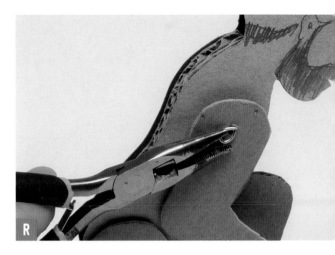

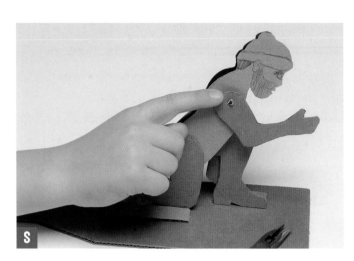

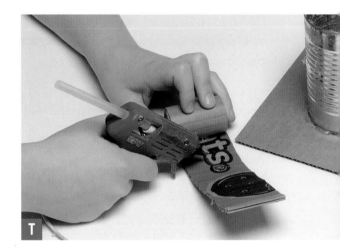

- Thread the right arm onto the wire. The end of the wire is now all the way on the right-hand side.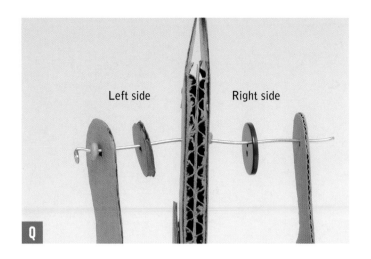

- **Adult Help:** Ask an adult to help you adjust and secure the wire. Trim the wire to about ½ inch from the surface of the arm using the cutter on your needle-nose pliers. With the tip of the pliers, grab the very end of the wire. While holding it securely, rotate your hand to form a little loop or circle in the wire. Grab that circle with the flat surface of the pliers blades to fold the wire. You want it to be parallel to the surface of the arm.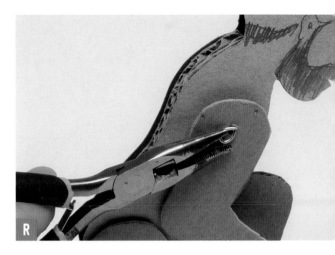

- Both arms should be attached snug to the body, but not so tight that they cannot easily move.

- Test the swing of the right arm. Make sure it moves freely. If it is too loose or too tight, adjust the wire loop on the right side.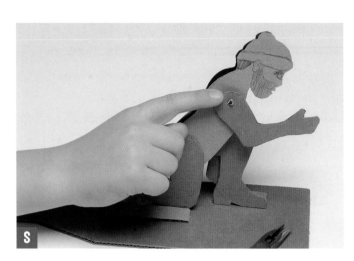

- **Adult Help:** Place the ax on the inside of the right hand, with the part that looks like a flag pointing down. Hot glue the ax to the inside of the right hand.

ROLL AND ATTACH THE LOG

- **Adult Help:** Take the 2 × 20–inch cardboard strip. Fold over one short end and roll it a couple inches. Put a dab of hot glue in the center of the flat bit of cardboard right in

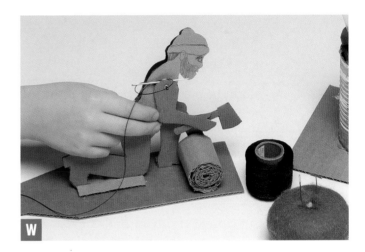

front of the roll. Then roll more of the cardboard onto the glue. Continue to glue and roll, glue and roll. Continue until the log is about 1½ inches in diameter. You may not need all the length you cut. Trim the cardboard when the log is that size. Make sure the edge is glued securely. **T**

- The strip should now look like a log. Place the rolled log onto the base. The left edge should be snug against the inside of the left toe. Don't glue it yet.

- Swing the right arm a bit. The ax should come down on top of the log without catching the handle. If it doesn't, move the log backward or forward a bit until the ax moves freely. Mark the log's position with a pencil. **U**

- **Adult Help:** Hot glue the log to the base.

- **Adult Help:** Bring the left arm forward to touch the left side of the log. Glue it in place. **V**

STRING THE WEIGHT

- Cut a piece of thread 20 inches long. Thread one end through a needle.

- Attach the thread to the right arm in this way, from back to front: Insert the needle at the "needle insertion" point at the upper edge at the back of the arm. Push it through the center of the cardboard, out through the front. Loop the thread back over to re-enter the back of the arm at the same place. After the thread has been looped through, place a dot of glue to keep the thread from pulling out. Trim any loose ends. **W X** (page 156)

- Use the ¼-inch punch to make the arm thread hole you marked on the base.

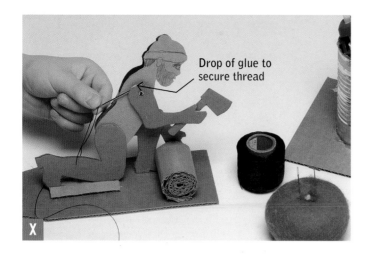

Drop of glue to secure thread

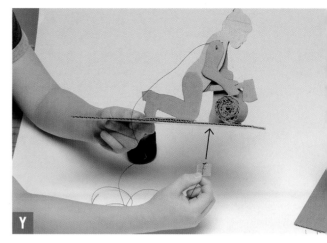

- Run the other end of the thread through the hole in the base. Leave it hanging below the base.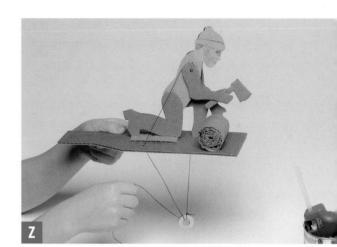

- Mark the position of the weight thread by poking a needle through the spot marked on the base, so that you can see where to glue the string underneath the base. Mark it with a pencil so you can see it better.

- Cut a piece of thread 20 inches long. Tie a knot in the end.

- **Adult Help:** Hot glue the knot to the ½–inch cardboard square. Hot glue the square to the bottom of the base where you marked it for the weight thread. (See Y)

- Tie the weight pendulum to the front thread so that it hangs 5 or 6 inches below the base. Cut off the extra string. Once tied on, the weight should hang straight down.

- Take the weight thread, hanging near the back underneath the base. Tie its end to the weight. It will attach at a slight angle and be slightly longer than the front thread.

Your Paul Bunyan logger is complete. Time to test its movement. Hold on to the narrow end of the base. Swing the base in a circle, in the direction a merry-go-round travels. The swinging weight will make the arm move up and down. It will look like Paul is chopping wood with his ax! Your Paul might not be as big as the massive statues found in Minnesota, but it is probably the only one that chops wood on its own! Have fun and chop away.

TWISTER TORNADO

Skill Level 4

Atmospheric vortex. Cycling supercells. Wildly rotating wall clouds. Rear flank downdrafts. These phrases sound like they're describing epic battles of superheroes! And perhaps, in a way, they are epic battles. But not between superheroes. These terms are describing battles between opposing masses of air. In this fight, low-level moist air from the Gulf of Mexico meets dry cold air from Canada head on. *BAM!* The cold air forces the warm, moist air upward, where it cools. But cold air can't hold as much moisture as warm air. So what happens to all that extra water? It condenses into clouds, and that's how a thunderstorm begins. If the winds are particularly strong and

Tornado near St. Cloud, Minnesota, 1909

start turning clockwise, look out! A funnel cloud may develop out of the swirling wind. The funnel cloud can reach down toward the ground. And once it touches the ground, a tornado is born.

Tornadoes are Mother Nature's bad boys. They are violent, rotating winds that can reach speeds of 300 miles per hour. They can rip apart a house in 15 seconds and send cars flying. The greatest number of tornadoes in the world occurs in the United States. More than a thousand tornadoes form in the United States each year, and the greatest number of those occur in the Great Plains area, a place known as "Tornado Alley."

There is an old saying, "Every cloud has a silver lining." This means that even when something bad happens, good things can come from it. A tornado is a really big, destructive cloud. How can anything good come from that?

Tornado near Bellingham, Minnesota, 1939

A silver lining *was* discovered in Rochester, Minnesota, long ago. It was August 21, 1883. Several tornadoes hit southeastern Minnesota. Thirty-seven people were killed. More than 200 others were injured. At the time, there were only three hospitals in the entire state that were outside the Twin Cities. None of these hospitals was near Rochester. So people injured from the tornadoes were transported to Rommel Hall in Rochester to be treated. That was a dance hall, not a hospital. A frontier doctor and his two sons went there to treat the patients, and they were helped by nuns from the Sisters of St. Francis. After the disaster ended, Mother Mary Alfred Moes asked these doctors to help build a permanent hospital in Rochester. The doctors were William Worrel Mayo and his two sons, William J. Mayo and Charles H. Mayo. St. Mary's Hospital opened in 1889. It eventually became the world-famous Mayo Clinic.

In this craft, you'll make a tornado that actually spins! It's an automaton. An automaton (plural, *automata*) is a mechanical toy, which is really a simple machine. Transfer energy from your hand—through parts you create—to a tornado. Turn the crank; the tornado spins.

There are many ways to make automata: some simple, some complex. Wooden automata are very sturdy and predictable, but saws and drills are needed to build them. Your automaton will be made of cardboard, wire, and wooden dowels. It is fairly simple to make, but does take time and patience. Read ahead for more on the process and fun results!

Tornado safety is very important. If you see threatening weather, stay alert. Listen for tornado sirens. If you hear one, find cover right away. If you are in a place with a basement, go there. If there is no basement, go to a room without windows. The room should be on the lowest floor you can get to. You can also get in a closet or bathtub. If you are outside, lie flat in a ditch. Cover your head with your arms. Talk to your parents about tornado safety and have a plan.

NOTE TO CRAFTERS

Kids: This is a skill level 4 project. It's a great family project, designed to be done with an adult. None of the steps are hard, but there are a lot of them! Ask for help as you need it. You will cut dowels, bend wire, and use hot glue. Be safe. It will be worth it when you amaze your friends and family with your very own tornado!

Adults: If you have constructed things, you know there are many ways to put the same thing together. We designed this toy and carefully sequenced directions and tips to eliminate as many variables as we could while using recycled, non-standard materials. It's not fun when a toy doesn't work at the end of a long process. If you are familiar with construction, feel free to improvise. We recognize that often the process is as valuable as the product.

Supplies

- ☐ **Adult Help:** 2½–inch circle, 3-inch circle, 1½-inch square, 1½ × 4–inch rectangle templates (page 206 or at www.mnhspress.org/makinghistory), copied or printed on card stock (see note page 8)

- ☐ Corrugated cardboard box, 8 × 8 × 7 inches (available at office supply or copy/shipping stores)

- ☐ ³⁄₁₆-inch-diameter, 36-inch-long dowel (found at hobby or craft stores; get the straightest one you can find)

- ☐ Bamboo barbeque skewer (found in grocery stores)

- ☐ Scraps of corrugated cardboard (ours was ⅜ inch thick)

- ☐ **Adult Help:** 25-foot spool of 18-gauge galvanized steel wire, or 18- or 19-gauge annealed steel (found at hardware stores)

- ☐ 2 paper drinking straws, ¼ inch diameter (standard size; available at craft and gift stores)

- ☐ 2 small rubber bands

- ☐ 2 thick rubber bands (like the kind used to wrap broccoli at the grocery store; ¼ to ½ inch wide and big enough to go around a 3-inch circle snugly)

- ☐ ¼ sheet 80-grit sandpaper

- ☐ 2 twist ties

- ☐ Styrofoam floral cone (one that is 3⅞ × 8⅞ inches is a good size; found at craft and floral supply stores)

- ☐ Needle-nose pliers

- ☐ **Adult Help:** Fine-tooth saw, like a hack saw

- ☐ Pencil

- ☐ Safety glasses

- ☐ ¼–inch hole punch

- ☐ ⅛-inch hole punch (available at craft stores)

- ☐ **Adult Help:** Sharp, pointed tool to make a small hole, such as small nail, drawing compass, or awl

- ☐ Scissors

- ☐ Utility scissors or kitchen shears

- ☐ **Adult Help:** Hot glue gun and hot melt glue

- ☐ Craft glue

- ☐ 14- or 15-ounce tin can

Optional Supplies

- ☐ **Adult Help:** Cow and House templates (page 206 or at www.mnhspress.org/makinghistory), copied or printed on card stock (see note page 8)

- ☐ Needle and thread

- ☐ T-square ruler

- ☐ **Adult Help:** Hobby or craft knife and cutting mat

- ☐ Decorative paper

- ☐ Paint or markers

- ☐ Pictures from magazines, photos, or drawings

OVERVIEW OF DIRECTIONS

There are a lot of steps involved in making the tornado. An overview is below. Read it to get an idea of what you will be creating during each major portion of the craft. Then get started with the detailed directions that follow.

- Prepare the box by cutting it and punching holes.

- Cut a dowel to form a crank handle, a vertical axle, and a horizontal axle.

- Cut circles, squares, and rectangles from cardboard scraps to make cams, washers, and a crank.

- Attach a straw and washers to the box to make sure that the vertical axle is secure and perpendicular.

- Glue circles. Attach to the axles (dowels) to make the moving parts that will spin the tornado. You will assemble the vertical one first and the horizontal one second.

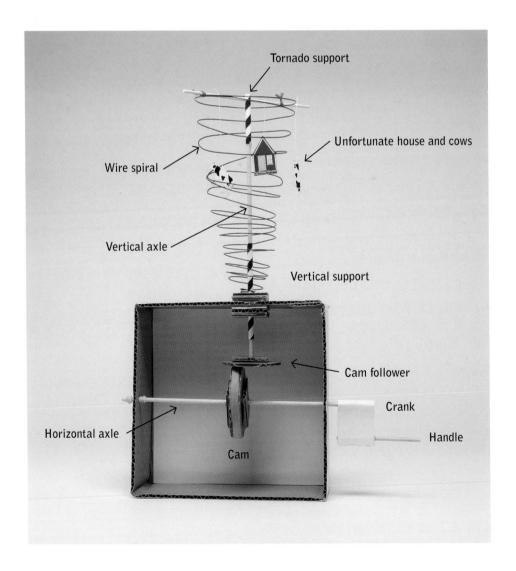

- Assemble and glue the top horizontal support that holds the tornado.

- Form a tornado from wire wrapped around a cone shape.

- Attach the tornado to the support.

- Optional: Decorate the outside of the box. Add some cows and a house.

- Turn the handle and watch the tornado come to life!

Directions

PREPARE THE BOX

- Fold up the flaps on one side of the box and tape them shut. **A**

    ✔ **TIP:** We cut our box in half. The toy's action is at the front, so you don't need as much depth. If you decide to cut your box in half, you end up with two boxes instead of one. Save one and make another automaton!

    ✔ **TIP: Adult Help:** To cut the box in half, set the box on its bottom. Measure 3½ inches from the bottom all the way around and mark a line. Cut along the line, or ask an adult to use a T-square and a craft knife to slice it instead.

- Set the box on its side so that the open part is facing you. Use a ruler to measure and mark a line on the top that is 3 inches from the right-hand edge.

- Insert the ¼–inch punch at this pencil line. Push it in as far as it will go (about ¾ inch) and punch a hole. Label this side "top." **B**

- On the right-hand side, measure and mark a line 4 inches up from the bottom of the box. Punch a hole on this line, just like you did the one on top.

- Repeat this step to punch a hole on the left side of the box. Set aside.

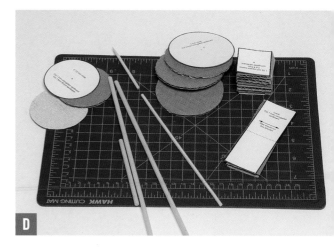

CUT THE PARTS

▨ Cut out the circle, square, and rectangle templates. Mark center points by punching a hole with the sharp-pointed tool. (Protect your work surface.) Trace the shapes onto corrugated cardboard as noted on templates. These pieces will be used for the "machine parts." Keep the templates with them after you cut.

> ✔ **TIP:** It's easier to cut rounded shapes from cardboard if you remove some of the extra cardboard around the shape first. Rough cut around the shape, and then cut accurately along the line. **C**

▨ This is what you need to cut from corrugated cardboard:

- Eight 1½ × 1½–inch squares

- One 1½ × 4–inch rectangle. This should be cut so the ribs (see page 7) of the cardboard run across the short end, not down the 4-inch side.

- One 2½–inch circle

- Three 3-inch circles. Be especially accurate as you cut these. They will be glued together to use for the part that spins the tornado. The more accurately you cut, the better the tornado will spin.

▨ Transfer template center markings with a pencil after you cut.

▨ Use utility scissors to cut one 2½–inch circle from 80-grit sandpaper.

▨ **Adult Help:** Measure and mark the wood dowel. You need two 11–inch pieces and one 3½–inch piece. Ask an adult to help you use a fine-tooth saw (like a hack saw) safely. Saw the dowels at your marks. (You may be able to cut them with a utility scissors.) Set them aside.

▨ Measure and mark a bamboo skewer 7 inches from the straight end. You can cut it with scissors. Discard the pointed leftover piece. **D**

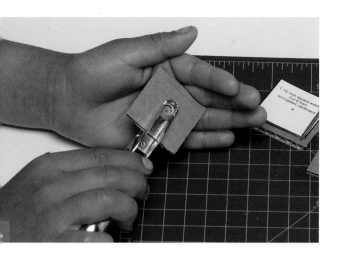

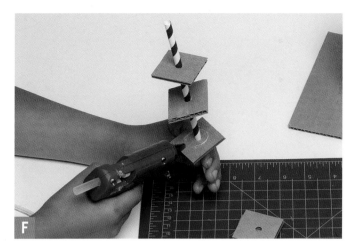

PREPARE THE VERTICAL AXLE SUPPORT

- Take five of the square cardboard washers you cut earlier. Use the ¼–inch punch to punch holes in the middle of each square at your center marks. Place three of the squares on a straw to keep them straight while you glue them together. Keep a bit of space between each. As you glue these together, be careful you do *not* glue the squares to the straw! Glue them to each other, one at a time, lining up the edges. **E** **F**

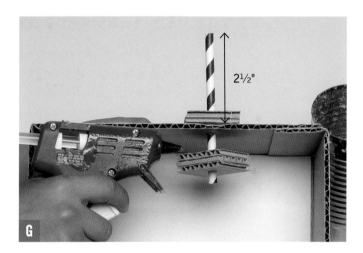

- Remove this set of washers from the straw and set aside. Repeat the process, only this time just use two squares. Remove and set aside.

- Measure and cut a 4-inch piece of the straw. Insert the straw into the hole at the top of the box. Leave 2½ inches of the straw sticking above the box. (See photo G) Squirt a generous amount of craft glue (not hot melt glue) around the base of the straw. This is the spot where it meets the box. The glue doesn't have to dry before you do the next part.

- **Adult Help:** Take the two-part washer and place it onto the straw on top of the box. Hot glue the bottom of the washer. Slide down and press to attach it to the box.

- **Adult Help:** Take the three-part washer. Place this one onto the straw *underneath* the top of the box. Hot glue the top of the washer. Press up on the washer to attach to the underside. **G**

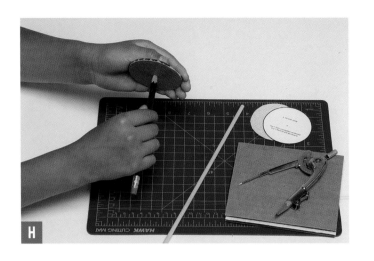
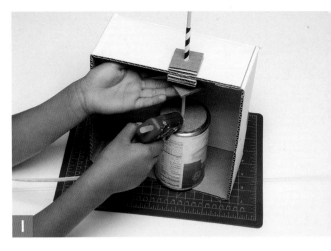

MAKE THE VERTICAL AXLE AND CAM FOLLOWER

Note: A *cam* is a machine part that moves another part. The part it moves is called a *cam follower*. In this craft, the crank will turn the horizontal dowel (axle) with its attached cam. That cam will then move the cam follower, which is attached to a vertical dowel (axle). The tornado is also attached to the vertical axle. See labeled photo on page 162.

- Lay down a doubled-over scrap of cardboard to protect your work surface. Lay the 2½-inch cardboard circle on top and use your sharp pointed tool to press through the middle dot all the way through the cardboard circle.

- Enlarge this hole with the point of a pencil *just enough* so that the dowel fits into it snugly.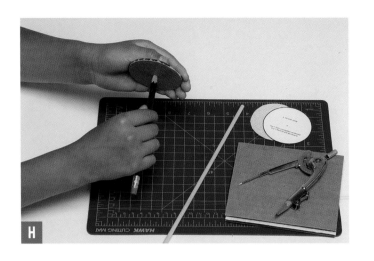

    ✔ **TIP:** Enlarge the hole a tiny bit at a time so that you don't make it too big.

- Cover the smooth side of the sandpaper circle with craft glue. Attach it to the bottom of the cardboard circle. Make sure the circle edges line up! Press down firmly to stick. Let the glue dry for a couple minutes.

- Take the 14- or 15-ounce can. Set it inside the box so its top is directly centered underneath the straw. If there is a pull tab on one side, turn the can upside down so the smooth end is facing up.

- Place the circle on top of the can, sandpaper side down.

- Take one 11–inch dowel. Insert it into the top of the straw. Thread one of the square washers onto the bottom of the dowel. It will be loose on the dowel as you do the next steps. (See relationship of parts in photo I.)

- **Adult Help:** Push the dowel down to make sure it will go into the center of the circle that's on top of the can. If the dowel doesn't come down straight into the hole, move the can and the circle until it does. It's important that the dowel stand as straight up and down as possible. Once it's in position, pull the dowel up and squirt hot glue into the hole of the circle. *Immediately* press the dowel down into the glue. Make sure the dowel is pushed down as far as it will go. Hold it for a moment until the glue cools.

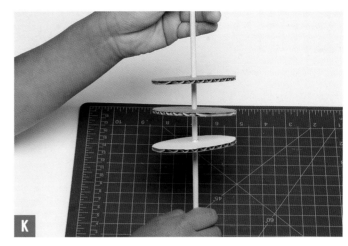

- **Adult Help:** Squirt a generous amount of hot glue around the base of the dowel where it meets the cardboard circle. *Immediately* lower the washer that is sitting above on the dowel. Press it down into the glue. Let the glue cool for a few minutes.

- Lift the top of the dowel up until the circle and washer go as far as they can. Wrap a twist tie around the dowel at the top of the straw. This will hold the circle piece up out of the way for the next steps. **J**

- Remove the can and set aside.

MAKE THE CAM

- Take the three 3-inch cardboard circles. Lay one circle on top of some scrap cardboard and poke a small hole all the way through each circle.

- Use the point of a pencil or an awl to enlarge each hole, just as you did before. Remember to enlarge them *just enough* so that the circles fit snugly on the dowel. After all three circles have holes, slide them onto the second 11–inch dowel. Leave a little space between each one. **K**

  ✔ **TIP:** This is a great time to ask another family member to help you glue the circles together by holding the dowel vertically. That way, you can glue with one hand as you turn the circle with the other. You'll have to work fairly quickly, so the glue doesn't cool before you get all the way around!

- **Adult Help:** Glue the circles together. Start with the bottom circle. Use a hot glue gun to run a line of glue on top of the circle, along the inside but not too close to the edge or to the dowel. You don't want glue to drip onto the outside edge, and you don't want the glue to be close to the dowel. Press the circle above this one down onto the glued surface. **L**

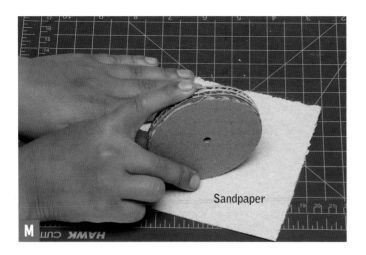

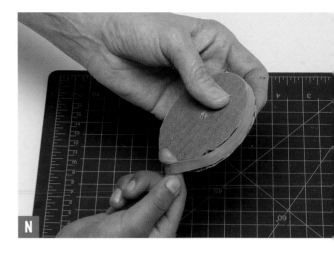

Repeat this step to glue the top circle to the other two. Now all three circles are glued together. This piece is the cam.

Remove the cam from the dowel. Run your finger along the edge. The three circles should line up with each other. If one of them sticks up above the others, gently sand the edge with a scrap of leftover sandpaper until they're even. **M**

Take a thick rubber band. Stretch it over the outside edge of the cam, like a tire. You may need help with this.

✔ **TIP:** If the rubber band is really tight, it may sink into the circles. If this happens, add another rubber band around the first one so that the rubber sticks out higher than the sides of the cardboard. That way the rubber will make good contact with the cam follower later on. **N**

CREATE THE HORIZONTAL AXLE

Now it's time to make the horizontal axle. Lay the 11-inch dowel down in front of you. Measure and mark 1 inch from the left side. Take a small rubber band and wrap it around the dowel on that line.

From the right side, thread a square washer onto the dowel. Then thread the cam and then another square washer.

Stand the box in front of you, with the open side facing you.

Want to learn more about automata? The Tinkering Studio has a great introduction on its website. This tornado automaton is based on some simple ones that its staff made with kids. The studio is inside the Exploratorium, a science and art museum in San Francisco. Visit http://tinkering.exploratorium.edu /cardboard-automata to find a link to the studio and an overview of cardboard automata! Other automata sites are shared there, too.

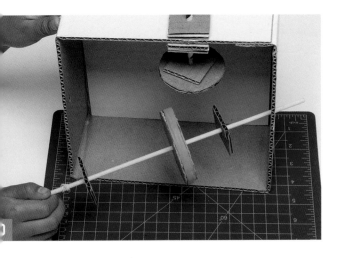

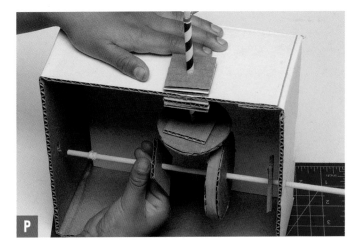

- Insert the right end of the dowel into the punched hole at the right side of the box.

- Now insert the left side of the dowel into the hole on the left side of the box. The rubber band will prevent the dowel from moving any farther to the left. P

- Take another small rubber band. Wrap it around the left end of the dowel that is sticking outside the box. The two rubber bands—one inside the box and one outside the box—will keep the dowel from sliding out of the holes. Make sure the dowel can still spin freely.

MAKE THE CRANK

- Take the 3½-inch dowel and the 1½ × 4-inch cardboard rectangle you cut earlier. You're going to make a notch in one of the short ends of the cardboard so that the dowel can fit into it. Use the scissors to make a slit along one of the ribs of the cardboard. Cut away enough of the top layer of cardboard so that the dowel can lay in the notch. Q

- **Adult Help:** Lay the cardboard in front of you like a piece of notebook paper so the two long sides are on the left and right. Place the notch toward the top end, away from you. Lay the dowel into the notch. Line up the left side of the dowel with the left side of the cardboard. Glue the dowel in place with hot glue. R (page 170)

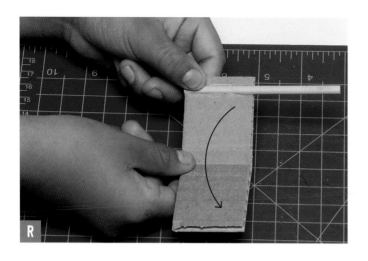

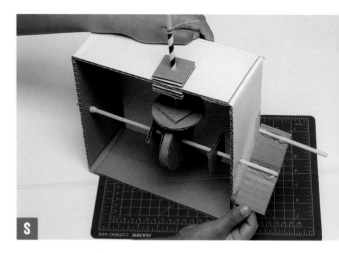

- Grab the dowel and bring it toward you to fold the rectangle in half. Crease along the folded line.

- **Adult Help:** Wrap the cardboard around the right side of the horizontal axle so the inside of the fold is against the horizontal axle. The handle should stick out the right-hand side. Line up the right edge of the cardboard with the right end of the axle. Open the cardboard and hot glue the axle into the fold. Use enough glue to make sure it's really stuck.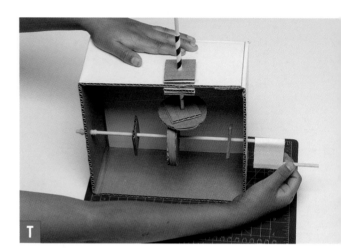

- Now hot glue the cardboard ends shut. Fold and press together.

- Now you have a handle, attached to a crank, attached to a horizontal axle, with a cam on it. It's beginning to look like a machine!

POSITION THE CAM

- Slide the cam along the horizontal axle until the rubber band edge is just under the left edge of the hanging cardboard circle. This hanging horizontal circle is called the cam follower. **T**

- Undo the twist tie from the vertical axle. Lower the dowel so that the cam follower rests on the cam.

- Crank the handle outside the box. When you turn the handle, the cam will spin. The rubber band should rub against the sandpaper on the bottom of the cam follower. This should make the cam follower spin.

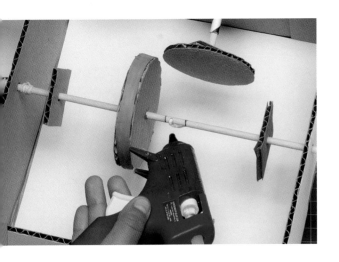
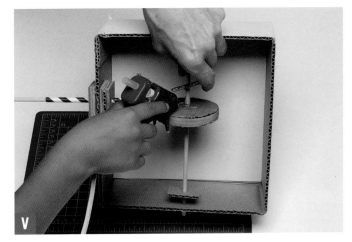

- If the cam follower is not spinning very well, check to make sure that the rubber band is touching the sandpaper. Adjust the rubber band if it's not. Slide the vertical cam to the left or right to get the best spin of the horizontal cam follower. Make sure that the cam is as straight up and down as possible. Those two adjustments should take care of any problems with the spin.

  ✔ **TIP:** If you ever accidentally glue something crooked with hot glue, use a blow dryer to warm the glue. The heat will soften it enough so that the glue joint flexes a little. Then you can adjust the part slightly.

  ✔ **TIP:** If you're still having trouble, you may have to take the rubber bands off the left hand of the axle and pull the axle out of the hole. Then you can try a different rubber band on the cam.

- Once the cam is where you want it, take a pencil and mark a line on the dowel on either side of the cam. Move the cam slightly to the left so that you see both marks.

- **Adult Help:** Tip the box so the open part is facing up. Add hot glue to the dowel between the pencil marks. *Immediately* slide the cam over onto glue. Make sure that the cam is perfectly straight up and down, not tipped to one side. It's okay if the cam pushes away some of the glue. **U**

- Start on the right side of the cam. You can turn the box so the right side is on top. That way the glue won't drip down. Hot glue around the base of the right side of the cam where it touches the dowel. Slide the square washer into the glue. Press the washer and cam together, but be careful you don't move the cam from its position on the dowel. **V**

- Turn the box again so the left side is on top. Repeat the last two steps to glue the left-side washer to the cam.

- Tip the box back up so the opening is facing you. Set the box aside.

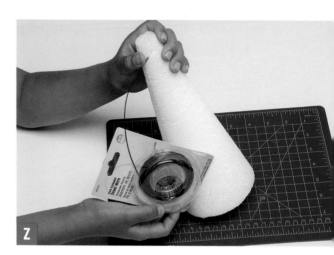

CREATE THE TORNADO SUPPORT

■ Make a "T-shaped" joint to hold the tornado support skewer. Measure and cut a 2-inch piece of straw. Take the ⅛–inch punch. Flatten one end of the straw and insert it into the punch to make a hole all the way through, a little more than ¼ inch down from the top edge.

✔ **TIP:** You may have to pull the punch's metal guard up a little in order to wedge the straw in there.

■ After punching, pull the straw out carefully so you don't rip it. Insert the tip of a pencil to open up the end of the straw again.

■ Take the bamboo skewer and push it through the hole so that it looks like a "T." Squirt a generous amount of craft glue into the top of the straw onto the skewer. Roll the skewer around to coat it in glue so that it glues to the straw. Make sure the straw is centered on the skewer. Set aside to dry.

CREATE THE TORNADO

■ Put on the safety glasses. Wire flops around easily and quickly. It's easy to get poked in the eye.

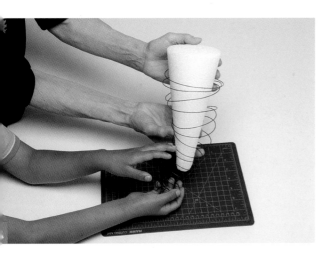

- **Adult Help:** Wrapping the cone with wire to create the tornado will require adult help. A second set of hands is a great idea!

- Take the floral cone. Set the wider flat end on the table. Pull a couple inches of wire out of its package. Use needle-nose pliers to make a ½-inch fold at the end of the wire so that there's not a sharp end. Squeeze it with the tip of your pliers to flatten.

- Push the folded end of the wire about ½ inch into the side of the floral cone near the top. This is to hold the wire while you wrap it. **Z**

- Wrap the wire in a spiral around the cone. One person can hold and slowly spin the cone and shape the wire as the other unravels and feeds the wire onto it. Space the lines out a bit. Wrap the wire securely, but not so tight that you won't be able to get it off the cone! You should end up wrapping the wire around the cone about 15 times. Stop wrapping when you reach the bottom of the cone.

- While one of you holds the cone and wire, the other cuts the end of the wire with the needle-nose pliers. Fold in the end about ½ inch and squeeze to flatten it.

- Pull out the wire end that is stuck in the top of the cone. Gently release all the wire from the cone. Don't pull too hard! You want to keep the spiral shape. **AA**

- Use a needle-nose pliers to round out the smaller end of the spiral.

ATTACH THE TORNADO

- Hold the wire spiral so that the smaller end is at the bottom. Place the wire spiral over the vertical dowel. The bottom curl of the wire should wrap loosely around the dowel and rest on top of the washer. Make sure it is loose enough to move. Adjust the wire a bit until it is. **BB**

- While one person holds the wire spiral in place, the other one will attach the T-shaped horizontal support. Spread craft glue over the top inch or so of the vertical dowel.

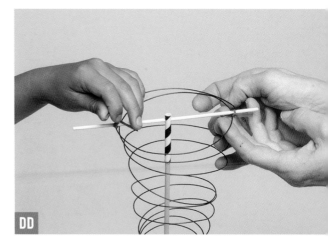

- Then put a dab of hot glue on the tip of the dowel. Lower the bottom of the T onto the top of the vertical dowel. Push down until the end of the dowel meets the skewer inside the straw. **CC**

- Squirt a little more hot glue into the top of the straw. Let cool. Use two clothespins to clamp the top curve of the wire to the skewer on either side of the straw. This will hold these pieces in position until you twist tie them together in the next step.

- Use two twist ties to connect the top curve of the wire to the bamboo skewer on either side of the straw. Make sure the wire spiral is centered on the vertical axle as well as on the horizontal skewer. Move it around a bit until it is. Make sure the twist ties are tight. **DD**

- Turn the crank to turn the tornado. Adjust the wire on the skewer if you need to. And now you're done!

- Optional: Decorate the box using any paint, stickers, or other decorations you gathered. Cut out the Cow and House templates. Fold in half and glue. Attach them to a thread with glue or a needle and hang them from the wires. Make an outdoor scene on the top of the box. What would a tornado be doing to the outdoors? Would trees be ripped up? Maybe you could even cut out copies of your own photos, and you can go flying!

Your tornado is complete. Surprise your friends and family. At first, keep the box opening faced toward you. When you turn the crank, people will be amazed as the tornado moves! Then you can show them the inner parts you created to make the movement possible.

Make another automaton, but think of other things to add to the vertical axle. Maybe you could make one with birds flying, or swings from a carnival ride. Instead of a long vertical dowel, cut a short one instead so you can attach a larger rotating disk in that place. What could you put on that?

Research automata to find out about other cam shapes and connecting mechanisms.

Fold

Fold

Fol

NORTH WOODS TROLL TEMPLATES

From *Making History: Have a Blast with 15 Crafts*, by Wendy Freshman and Kristin Jansson, © 2014. Published by the Minnesota Historical Society Press, www.mnhspress.org.

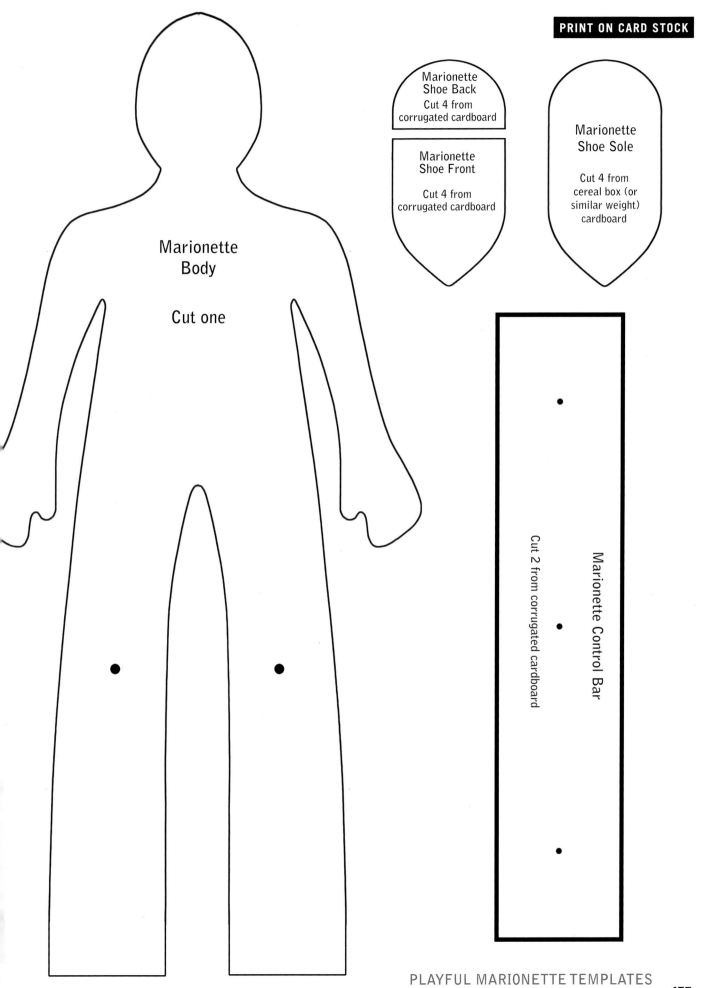

Marionette
Shoe Back
Cut 4 from
corrugated cardboard

Marionette
Shoe Front

Cut 4 from
corrugated cardboard

Marionette
Shoe Sole

Cut 4 from
cereal box (or
similar weight)
cardboard

Marionette
Body

Cut one

Cut 2 from corrugated cardboard

Marionette Control Bar

From *Making History: Have a Blast with 15 Crafts*, by Wendy Freshman and Kristin Jansson, © 2014. Published by the Minnesota Historical Society Press, www.mnhspress.org.

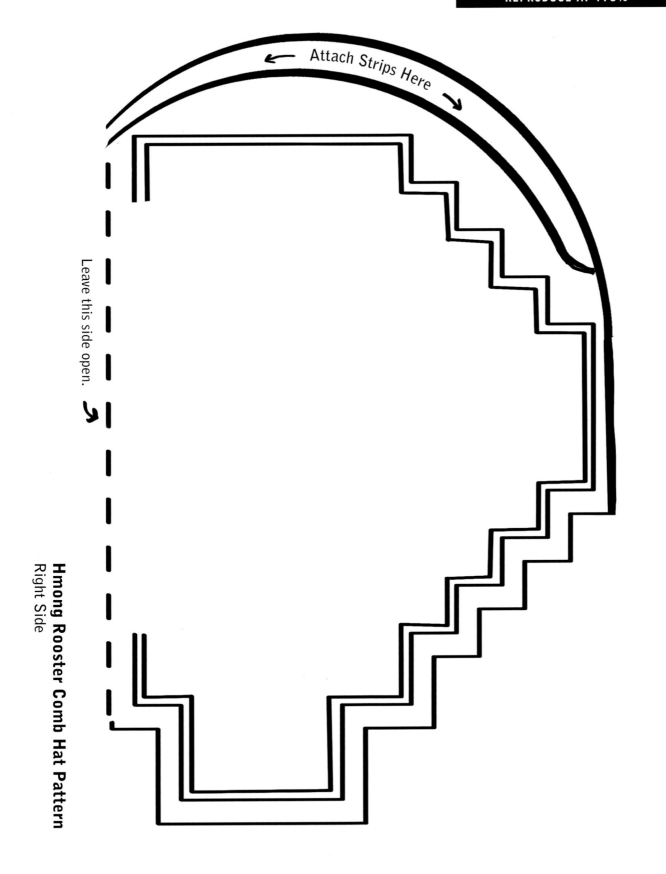

← Attach Strips Here ↘

Leave this side open. ↵

Hmong Rooster Comb Hat Pattern
Right Side

HMONG ROOSTER COMB HAT TEMPLATES

179

From *Making History: Have a Blast with 15 Crafts*, by Wendy Freshman and Kristin Jansson, © 2014. Published by the Minnesota Historical Society Press, www.mnhspress.org.

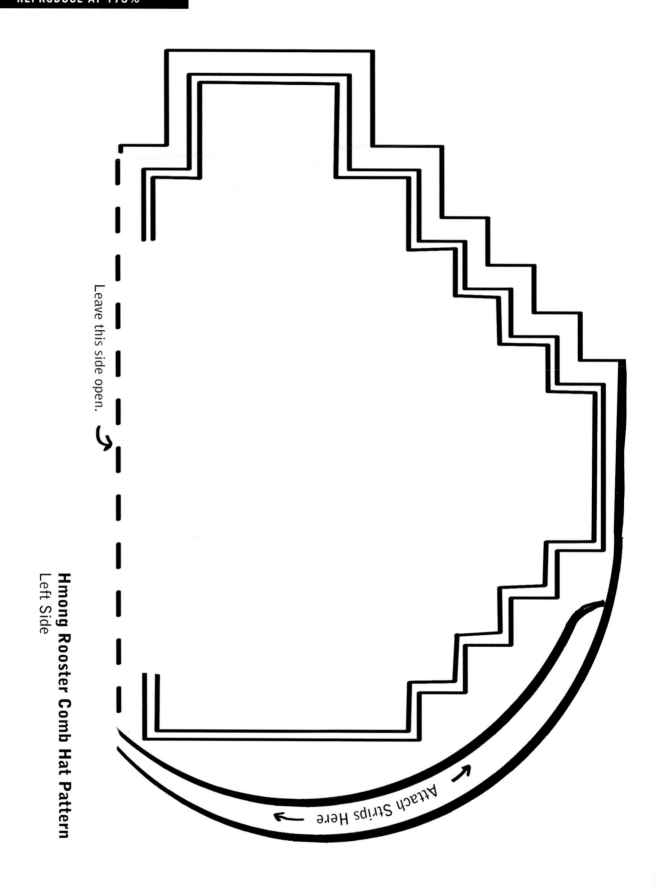

Leave this side open. ↶

Hmong Rooster Comb Hat Pattern
Left Side

Attach Strips Here

From *Making History: Have a Blast with 15 Crafts*, by Wendy Freshman and Kristin Jansson, © 2014. Published by the Minnesota Historical Society Press, www.mnhspress.org.

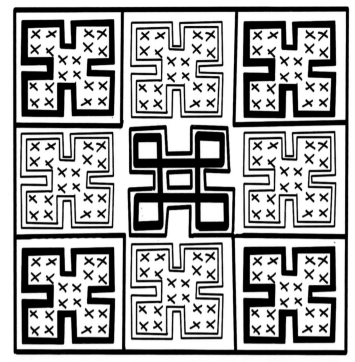

HMONG ROOSTER COMB HAT TEMPLATES

From *Making History: Have a Blast with 15 Crafts*, by Wendy Freshman and Kristin Jansson, © 2014. Published by the Minnesota Historical Society Press, www.mnhspress.org.

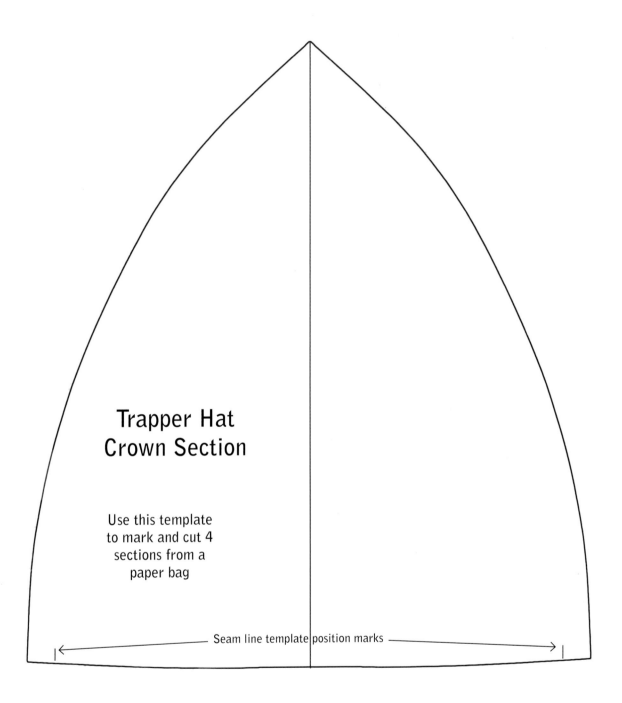

Trapper Hat
Crown Section

Use this template
to mark and cut 4
sections from a
paper bag

←———— Seam line template position marks ————→

From *Making History: Have a Blast with 15 Crafts*, by Wendy Freshman and Kristin Jansson, © 2014. Published by the Minnesota Historical Society Press, www.mnhspress.org.

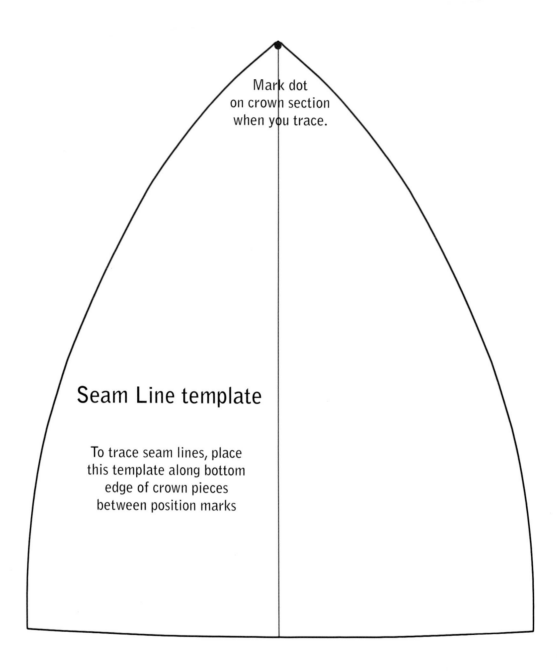

Mark dot
on crown section
when you trace.

Seam Line template

To trace seam lines, place
this template along bottom
edge of crown pieces
between position marks

From *Making History: Have a Blast with 15 Crafts*, by Wendy Freshman and Kristin Jansson, © 2014. Published by the Minnesota Historical Society Press, www.mnhspress.org.

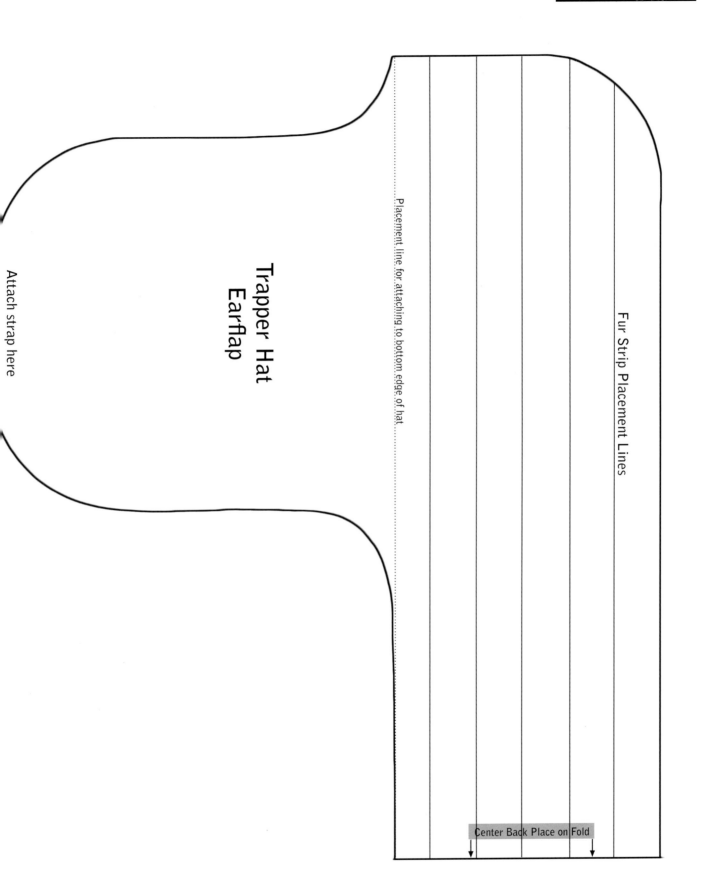

Attach strap here

Trapper Hat
Earflap

Placement line for attaching to bottom edge of hat.

Fur Strip Placement Lines

Center Back Place on Fold

MINNESOTA TRAPPER HAT TEMPLATES

From *Making History: Have a Blast with 15 Crafts*, by Wendy Freshman and Kristin Jansson, © 2014. Published by the Minnesota Historical Society Press, www.mnhspress.org.

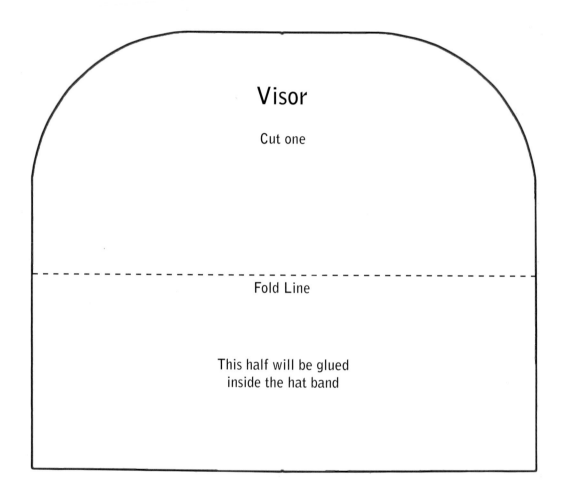

Visor

Cut one

- -

Fold Line

This half will be glued
inside the hat band

From *Making History: Have a Blast with 15 Crafts*, by Wendy Freshman and Kristin Jansson, © 2014. Published by the Minnesota Historical Society Press, www.mnhspress.org.

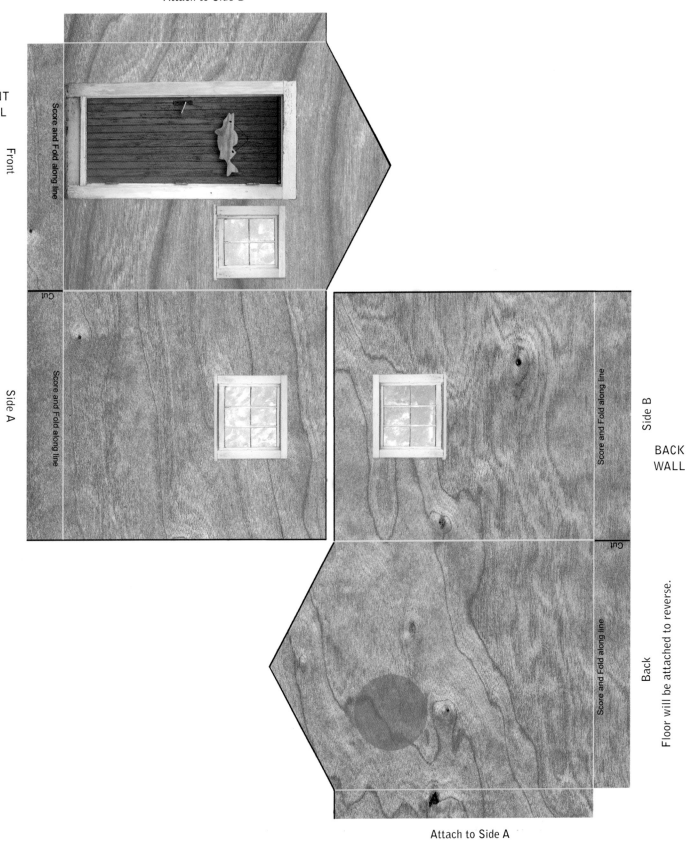

Attach to Side B

NT
L

Front

Side A

Score and Fold along line

Score and Fold along line

Cut

Attach to Side B

Side B

BACK
WALL

Score and Fold along line

Cut

Back

Score and Fold along line

Floor will be attached to reverse.

Attach to Side A

"GONE FISHING" ICE HOUSE TEMPLATES

From *Making History: Have a Blast with 15 Crafts*, by Wendy Freshman and Kristin Jansson, © 2014. Published by the Minnesota Historical Society Press, www.mnhspress.org.

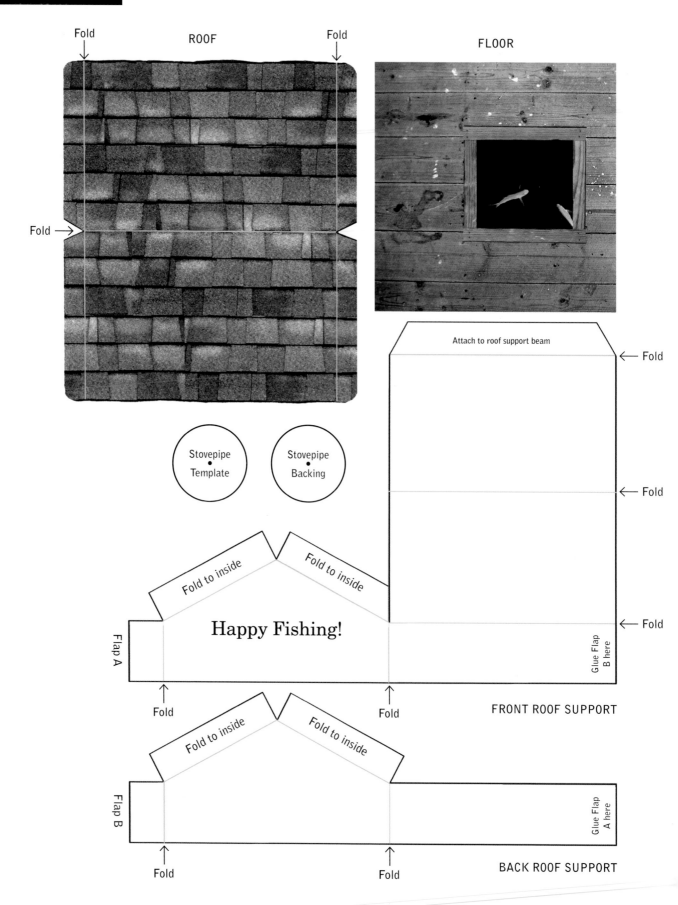

ROOF

Fold   Fold

Fold →

FLOOR

Attach to roof support beam

← Fold

← Fold

← Fold

Stovepipe
•
Template

Stovepipe
•
Backing

Fold to inside

Fold to inside

Happy Fishing!

Flap A

Glue Flap
B here

↑
Fold

↑
Fold

FRONT ROOF SUPPORT

Fold to inside

Fold to inside

Flap B

Glue Flap
A here

↑
Fold

↑
Fold

BACK ROOF SUPPORT

"GONE FISHING" ICE HOUSE TEMPLATES

From *Making History: Have a Blast with 15 Crafts*, by Wendy Freshman and Kristin Jansson, © 2014. Published by the Minnesota Historical Society Press, www.mnhspress.org.

Cobweb Front

From *Making History: Have a Blast with 15 Crafts*, by Wendy Freshman and Kristin Jansson, © 2014. Published by the Minnesota Historical Society Press, www.mnhspress.org.

Cobweb Back

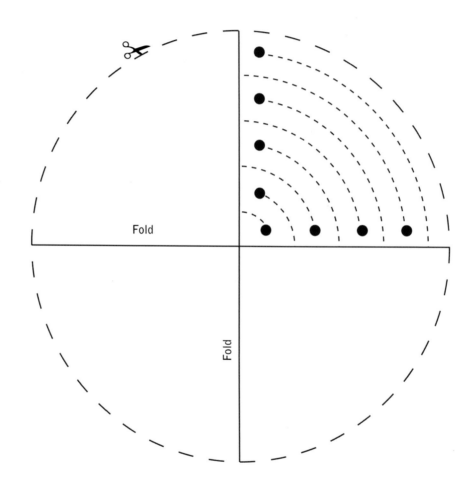

Fold

Fold

From *Making History: Have a Blast with 15 Crafts*, by Wendy Freshman and Kristin Jansson, © 2014. Published by the Minnesota Historical Society Press, www.mnhspress.org.

Base

From *Making History: Have a Blast with 15 Crafts*, by Wendy Freshman and Kristin Jansson, © 2014. Published by the Minnesota Historical Society Press, www.mnhspress.org.

Inner Circle Base

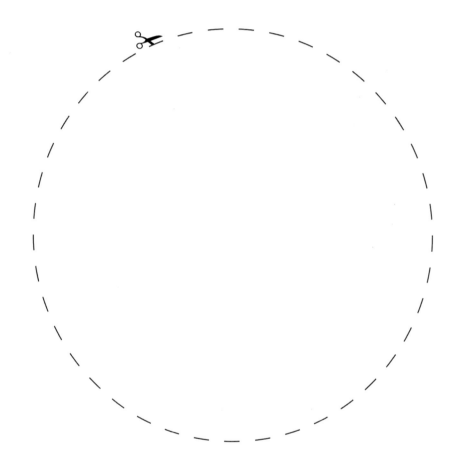

From *Making History: Have a Blast with 15 Crafts*, by Wendy Freshman and Kristin Jansson, © 2014. Published by the Minnesota Historical Society Press, www.mnhspress.org.

Valentine...
Let's make
history!

VALENTINE...
OUR LOVE IS
TIMELESS!

Valentine...
You have the key
to my heart!

Valentine...
We have a past,
let's make a future!

Envelope Template

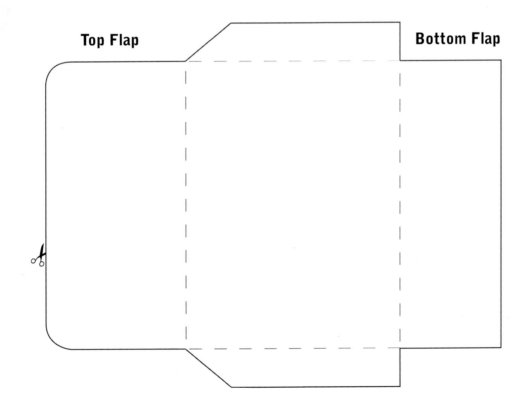

Top Flap

Bottom Flap

COBWEB VALENTINE TEMPLATES

From *Making History: Have a Blast with 15 Crafts*, by Wendy Freshman and Kristin Jansson, © 2014. Published by the Minnesota Historical Society Press, www.mnhspress.org.

DÍA DE LOS MUERTOS NICHO TEMPLATES

From *Making History: Have a Blast with 15 Crafts*, by Wendy Freshman and Kristin Jansson, © 2014. Published by the Minnesota Historical Society Press, www.mnhspress.org.

BATTERY BOX

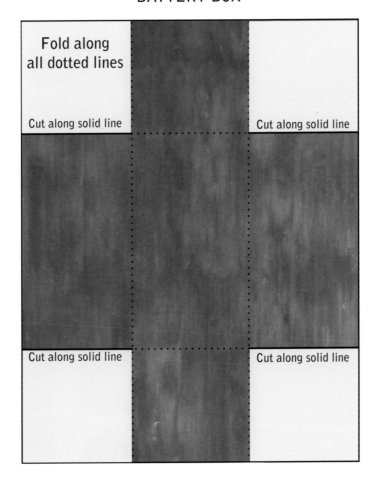

Fold along
all dotted lines

Cut along solid line

Cut along solid line

Cut along solid line

Cut along solid line

BENCHES

A

B

C

D

"RIDE THE WAVES" BOAT AND SKIER TEMPLATES

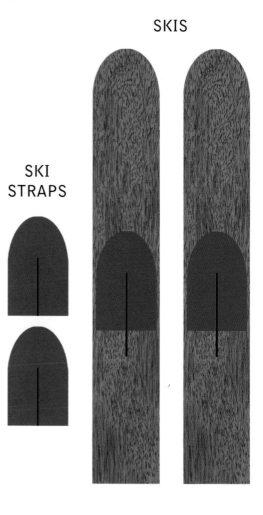

SKIS

SKI
STRAPS

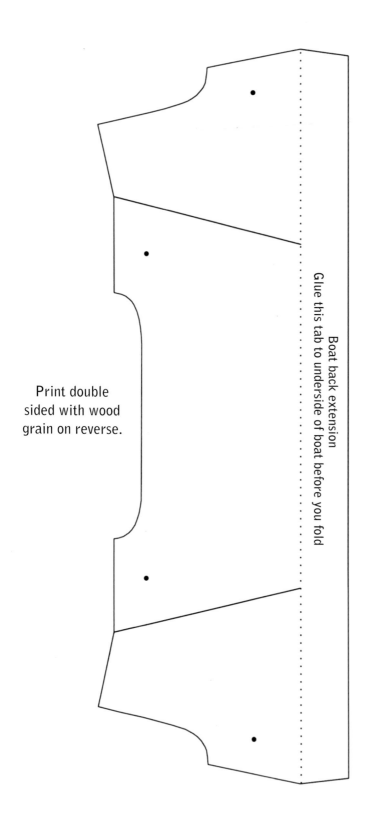

Print double
sided with wood
grain on reverse.

Boat back extension
Glue this tab to underside of boat before you fold

"RIDE THE WAVES" BOAT AND SKIER TEMPLATES

From *Making History: Have a Blast with 15 Crafts*, by Wendy Freshman and Kristin Jansson, © 2014. Published by the Minnesota Historical Society Press, www.mnhspress.org.

BOAT EXTERIOR

Print double
sided with wood
grain on reverse.

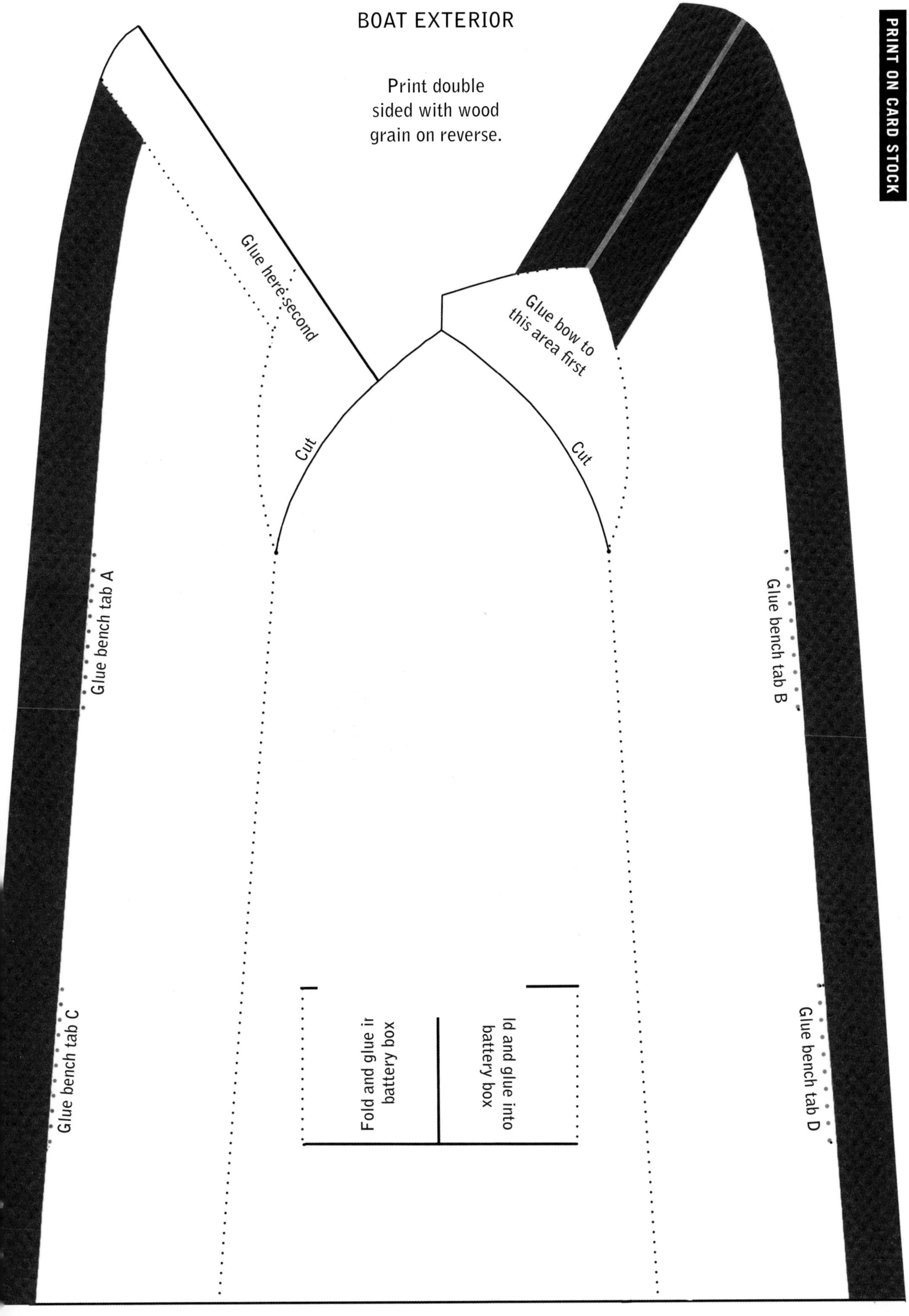

Glue here second

Glue bow to
this area first

Cut

Cut

Glue bench tab A

Glue bench tab B

Glue bench tab C

Glue bench tab D

Fold and glue ir
battery box

ld and glue into
battery box

RAMP EXTENSION

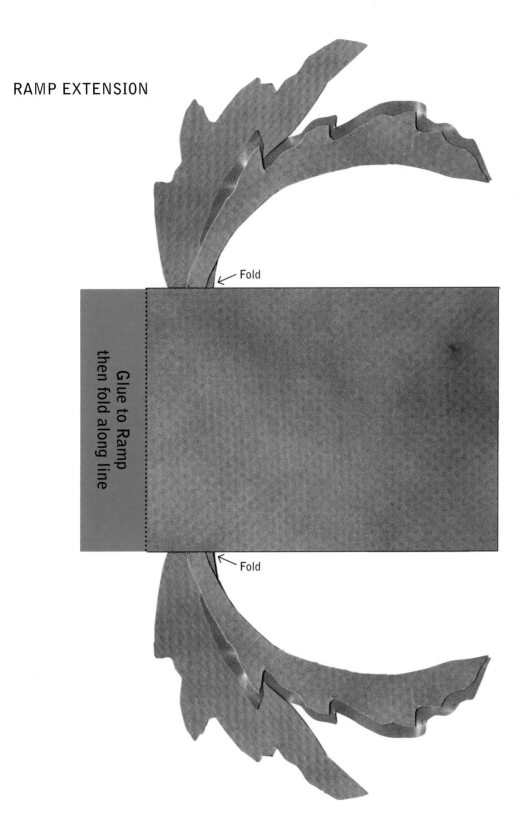

Fold

Glue to Ramp
then fold along line

Fold

"RIDE THE WAVES" BOAT AND SKIER TEMPLATES

From *Making History: Have a Blast with 15 Crafts*, by Wendy Freshman and Kristin Jansson, © 2014. Published by the Minnesota Historical Society Press, www.mnhspress.org.

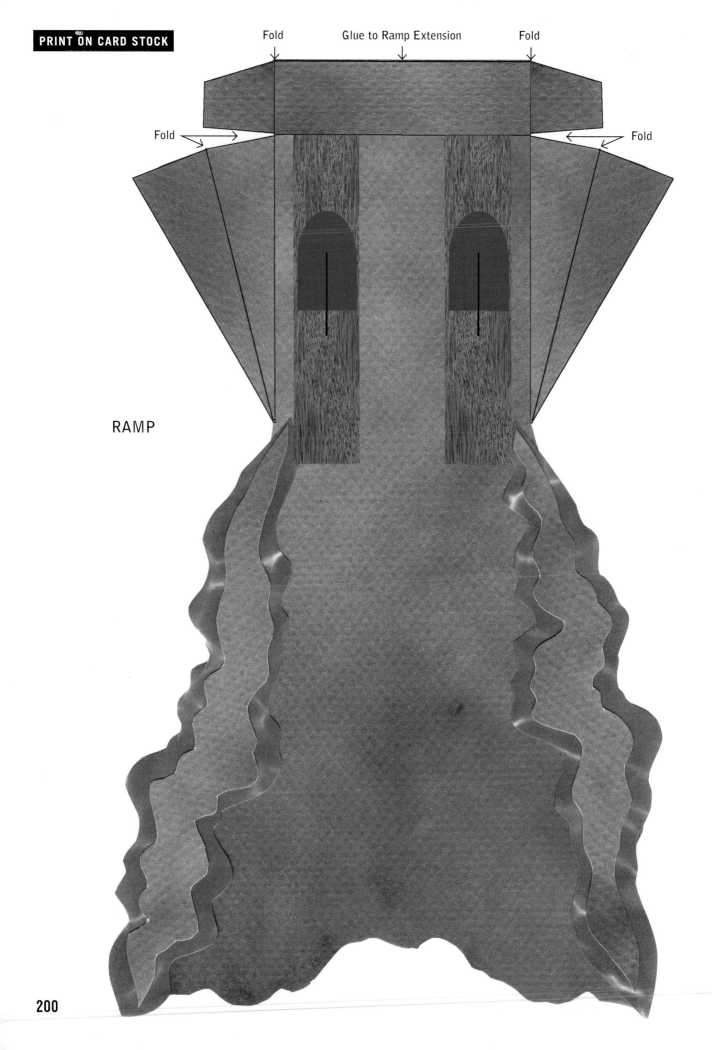

Fold

Glue to Ramp Extension

Fold

Fold

Fold

RAMP

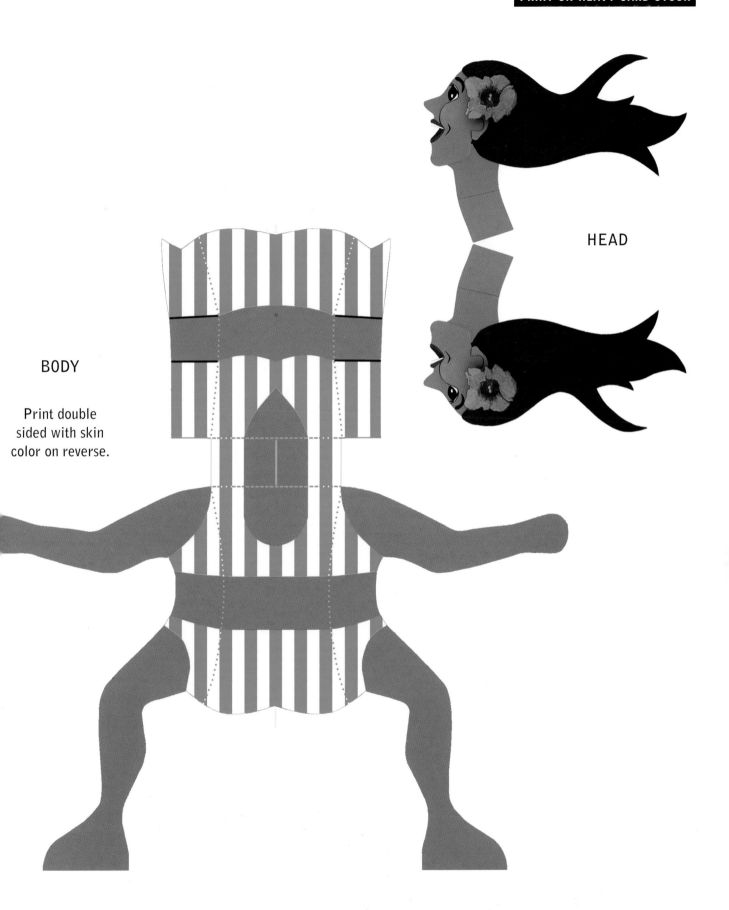

HEAD

BODY

Print double
sided with skin
color on reverse.

"RIDE THE WAVES" BOAT AND SKIER TEMPLATES

From *Making History: Have a Blast with 15 Crafts*, by Wendy Freshman and Kristin Jansson, © 2014. Published by the Minnesota Historical Society Press, www.mnhspress.org.

WATER-SKIER REVERSE SIDE

CARDBOARD PAUL

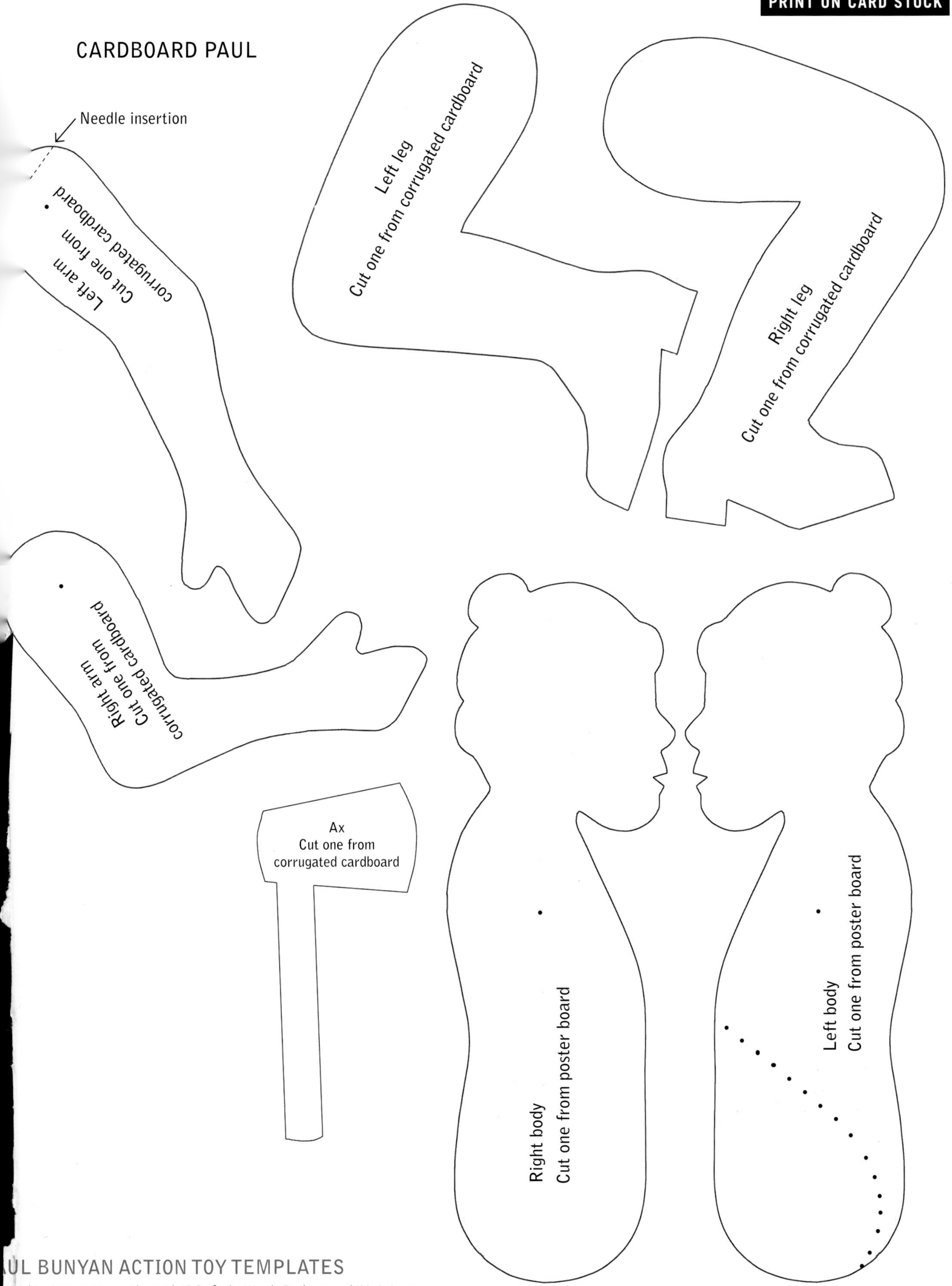

Needle insertion

Left arm
Cut one from
corrugated cardboard

Left leg
Cut one from corrugated cardboard

Right leg
Cut one from corrugated cardboard

Right arm
Cut one from
corrugated cardboard

Ax
Cut one from
corrugated cardboard

Right body
Cut one from poster board

Left body
Cut one from poster board

PAUL BUNYAN ACTION TOY TEMPLATES

From *Making History: Have a Blast with 15 Crafts*, by Wendy Freshman and Kristin Jansson, 2014. Published by the Minnesota Historical Society Press, www.mnhspress.org.

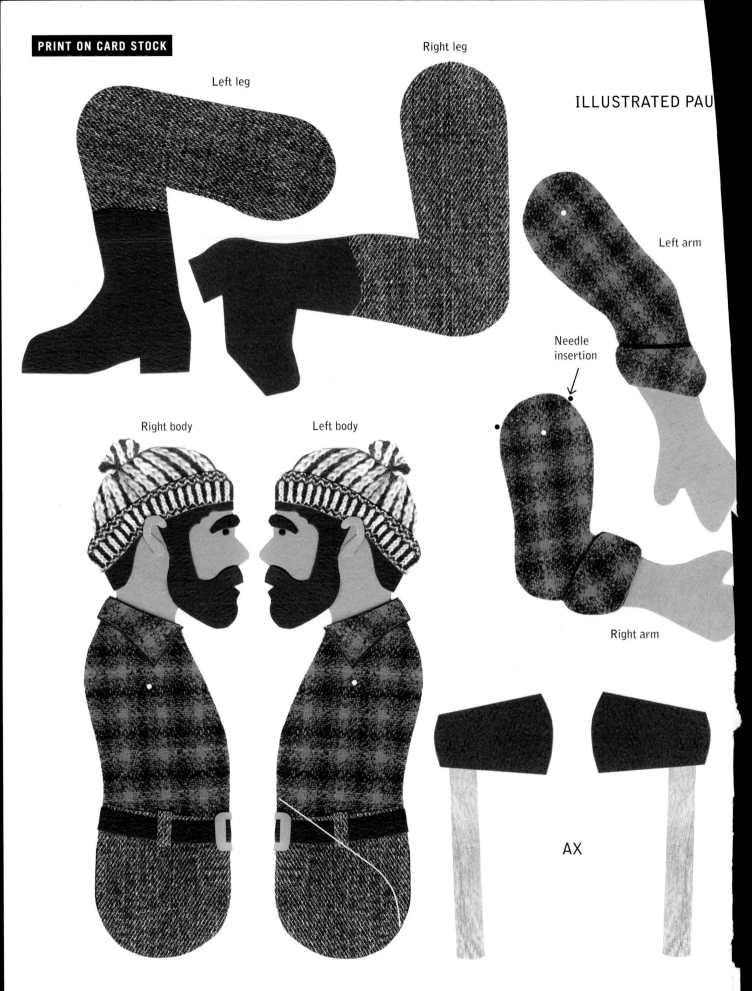

Left leg

Right leg

ILLUSTRATED PAU

Left arm

Needle
insertion

Right arm

Right body

Left body

AX

PAUL BUNYAN ACTION TOY TEMPLATES

 From *Making History: Have a Blast with 15 Crafts*, by Wendy Freshman and Kristin Jansson, © 2014. Published by the Minnesota Historical Society Press, www.mnhspress.org.

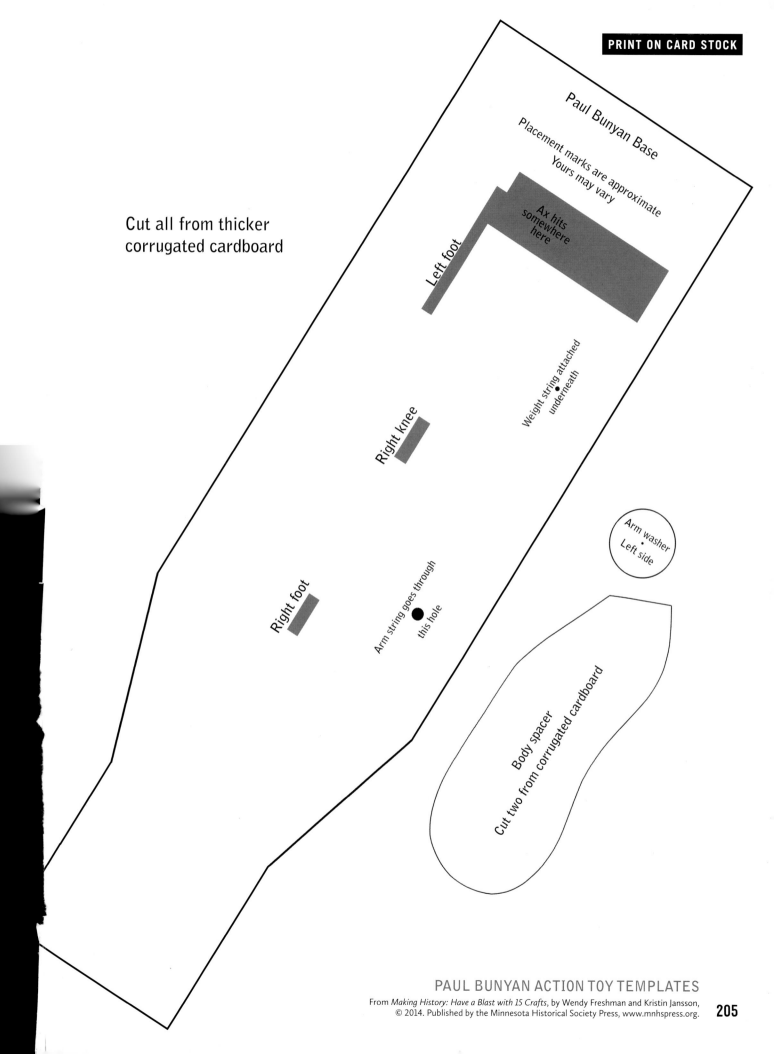

PRINT ON CARD STOCK

Paul Bunyan Base

Placement marks are approximate
Yours may vary

Cut all from thicker corrugated cardboard

Left foot

Ax hits somewhere here

Weight string attached underneath

Right knee

Arm washer
Left side

Right foot

Arm string goes through this hole

Body spacer
Cut two from corrugated cardboard

PAUL BUNYAN ACTION TOY TEMPLATES

From *Making History: Have a Blast with 15 Crafts*, by Wendy Freshman and Kristin Jansson, © 2014. Published by the Minnesota Historical Society Press, www.mnhspress.org.

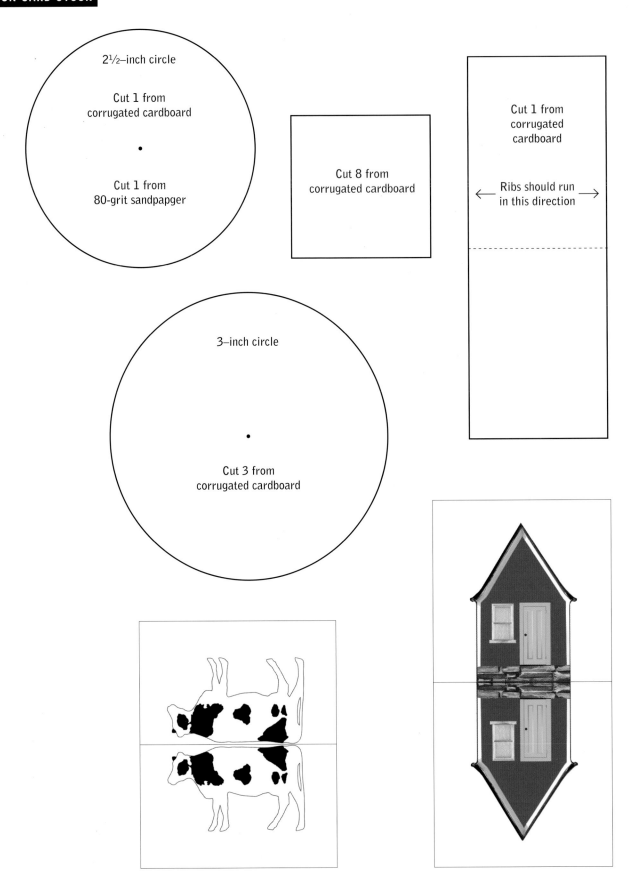

2½–inch circle

Cut 1 from
corrugated cardboard

•

Cut 1 from
80-grit sandpapger

Cut 8 from
corrugated cardboard

Cut 1 from
corrugated
cardboard

← Ribs should run →
in this direction

3–inch circle

•

Cut 3 from
corrugated cardboard